THE ADVENTURES OF ODYSSEUS AND THE TALE OF TROY

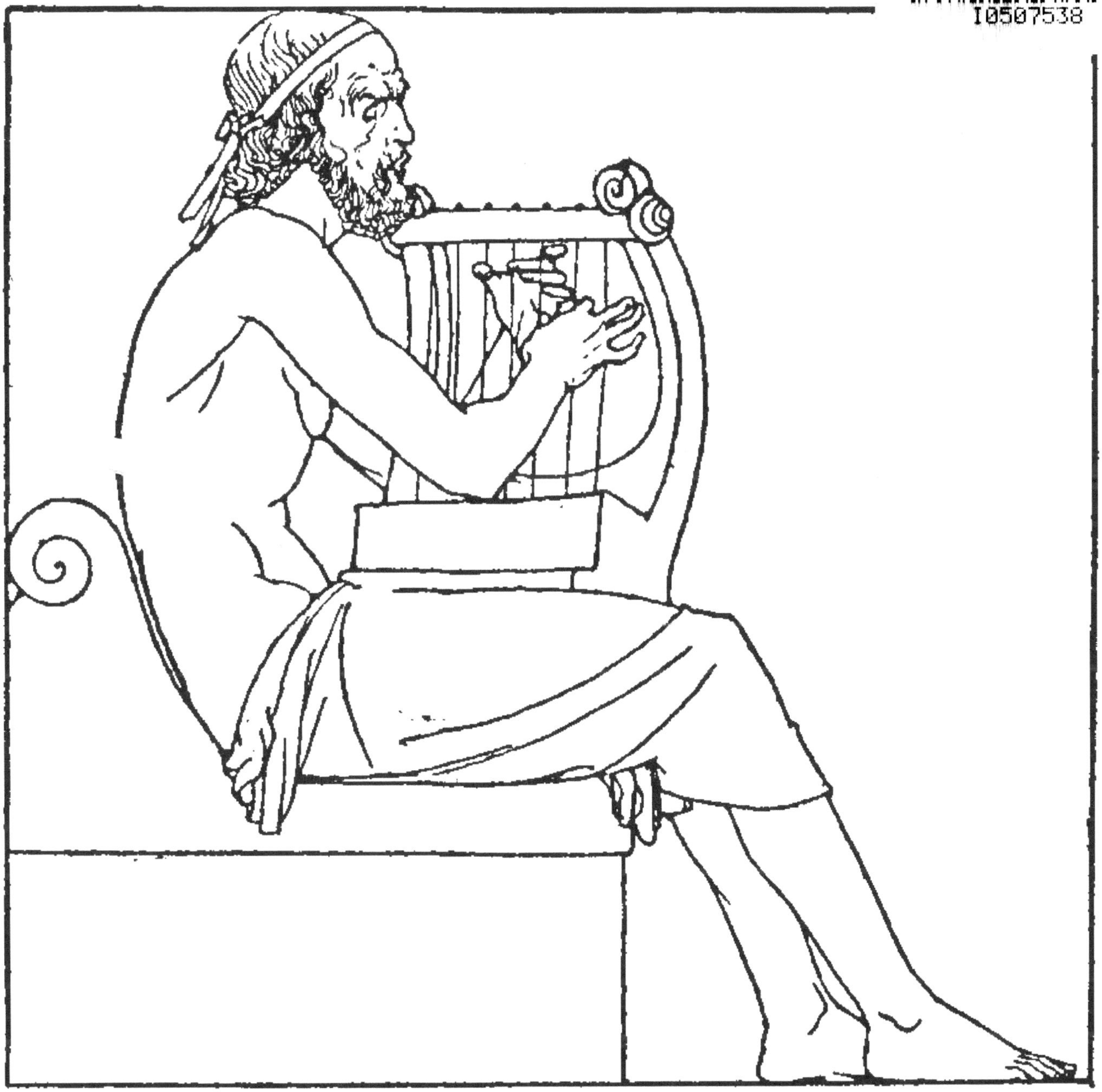

PRESENTED BY WILLY POGÁNY

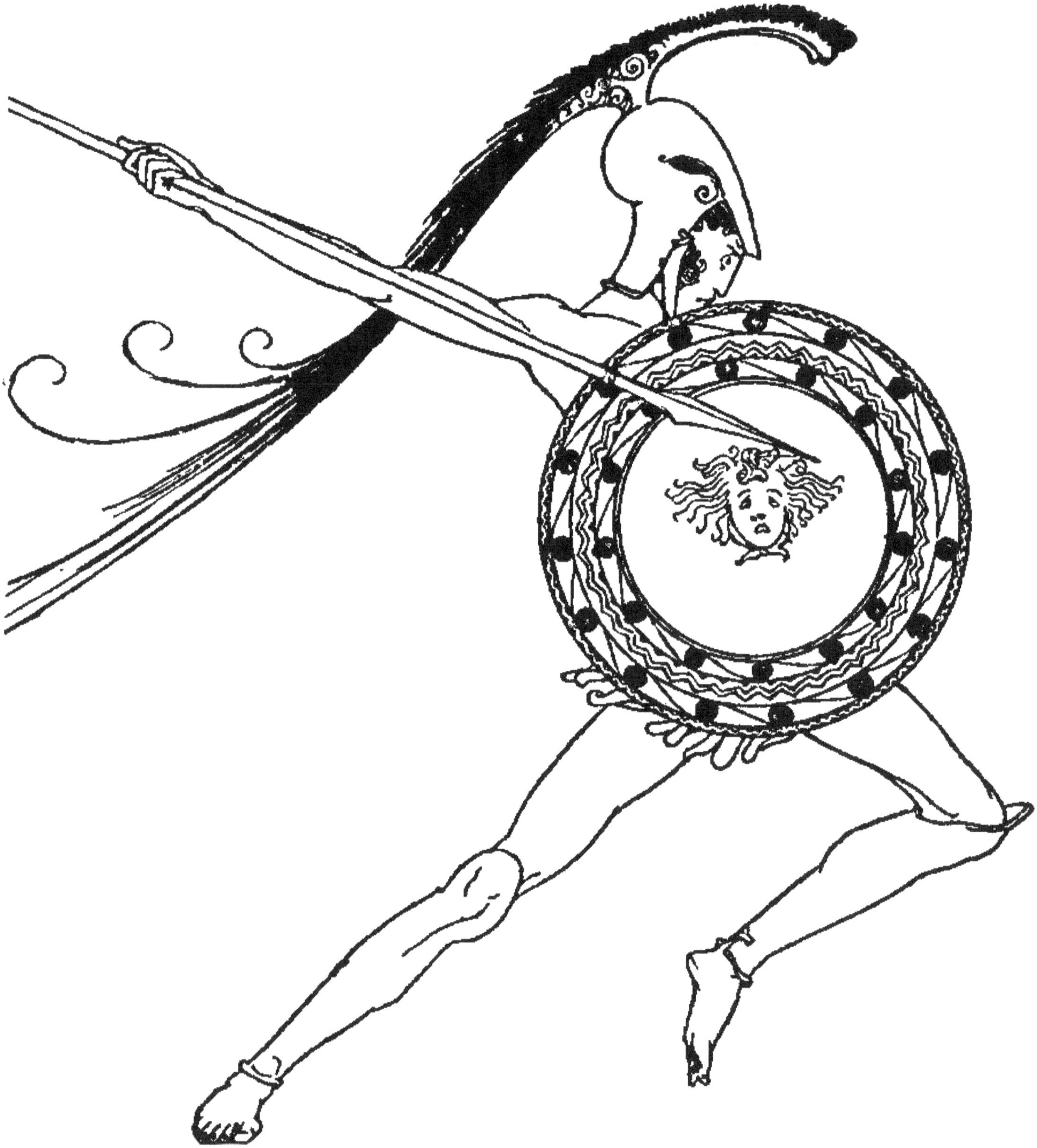

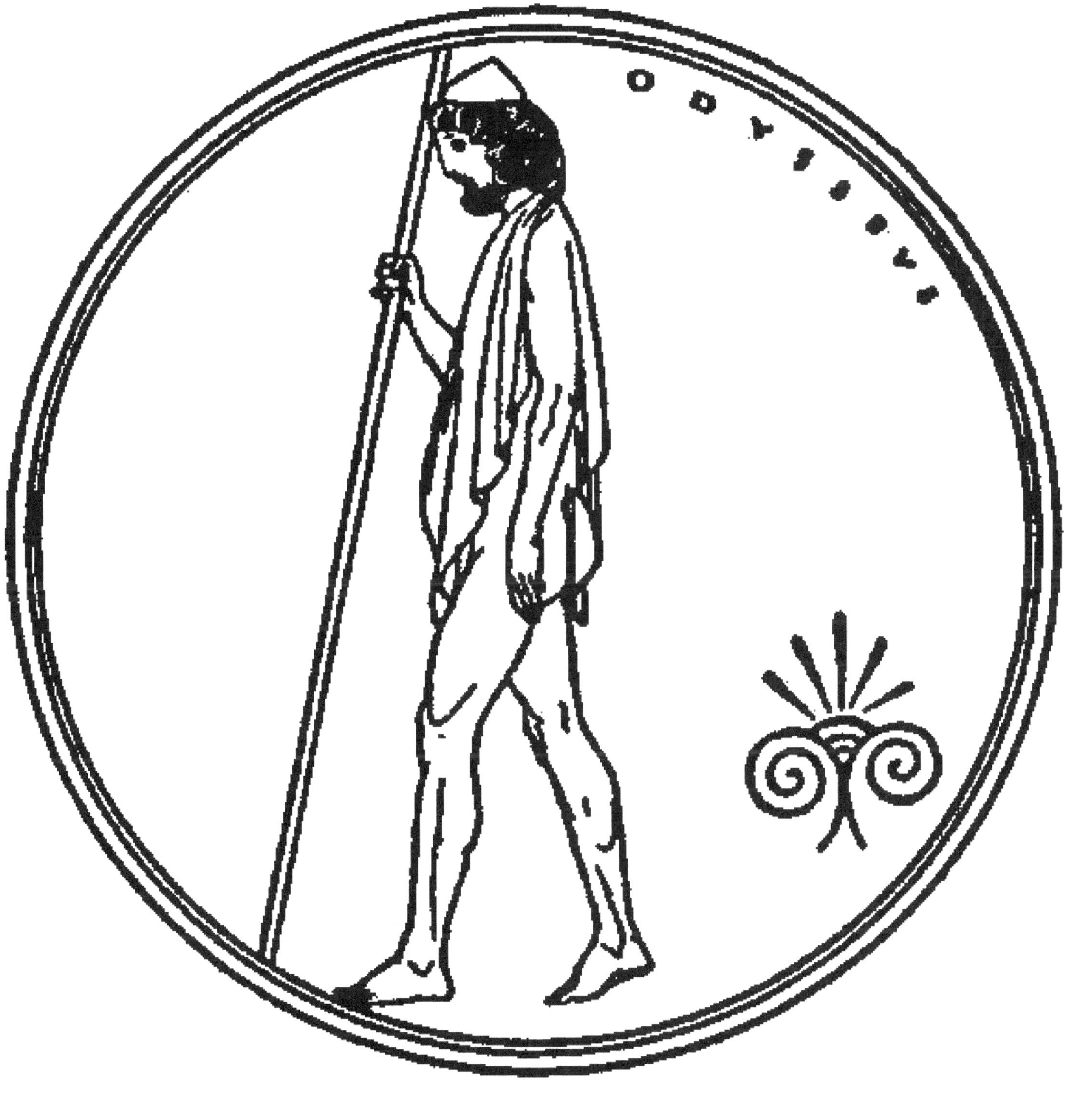

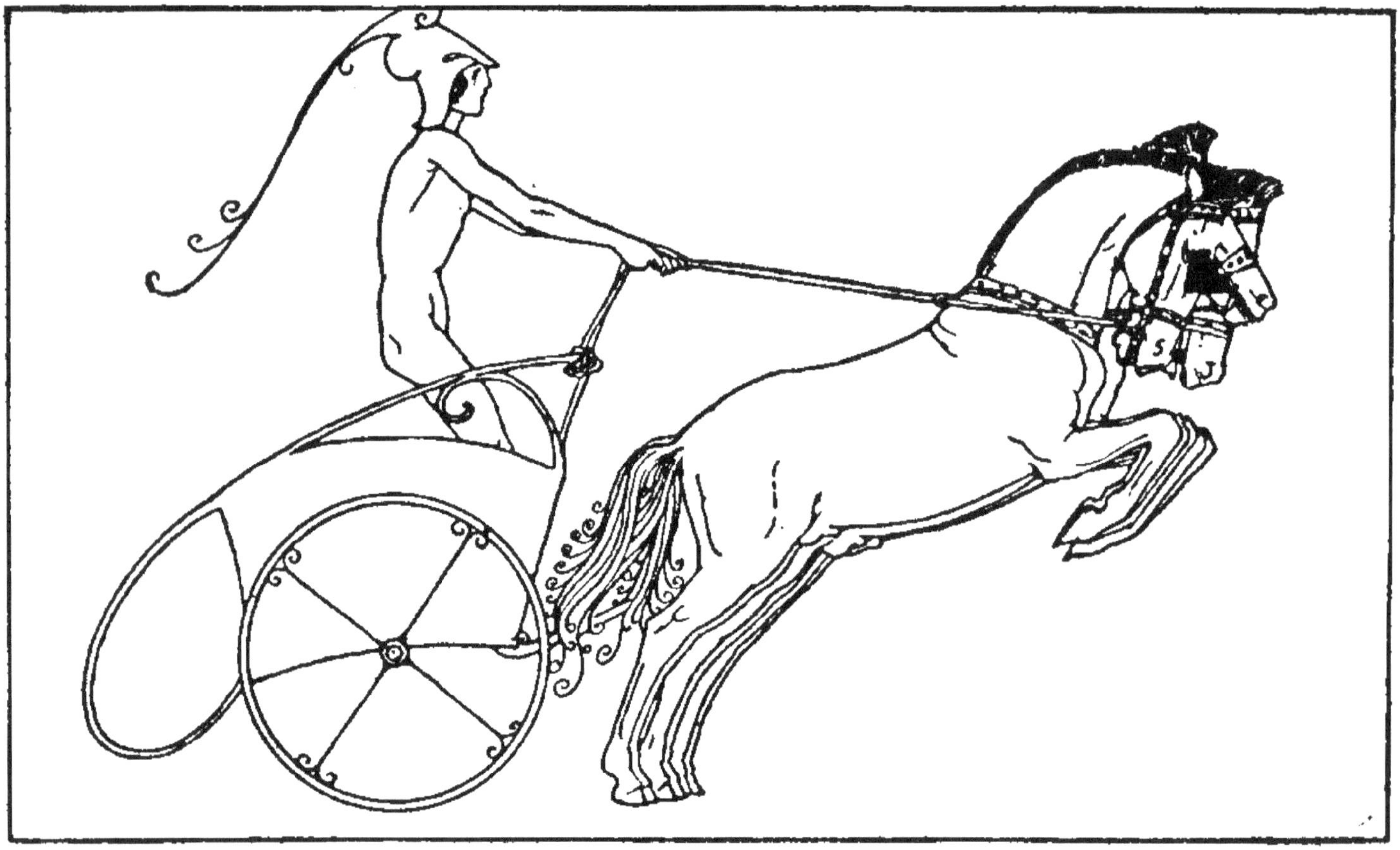

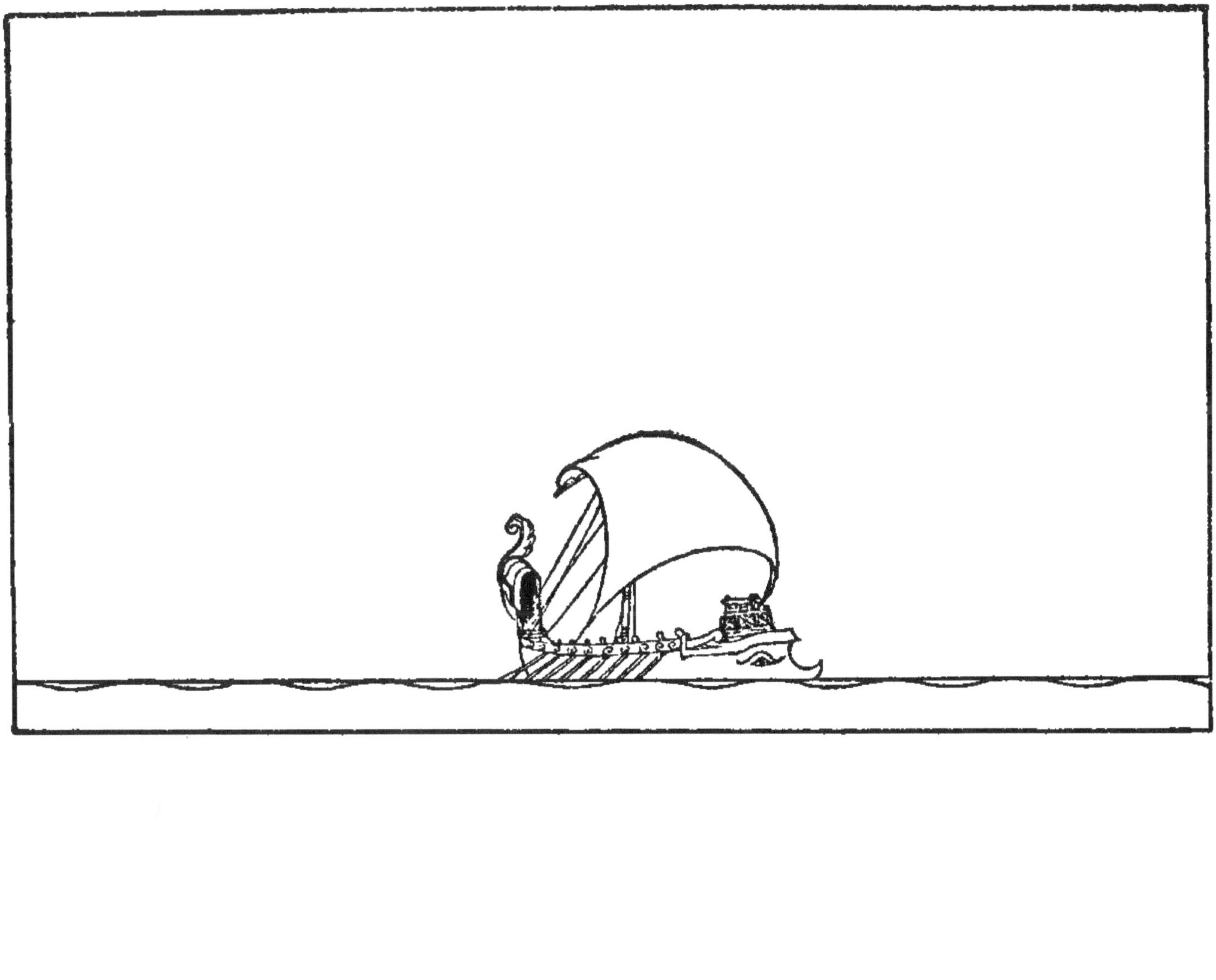

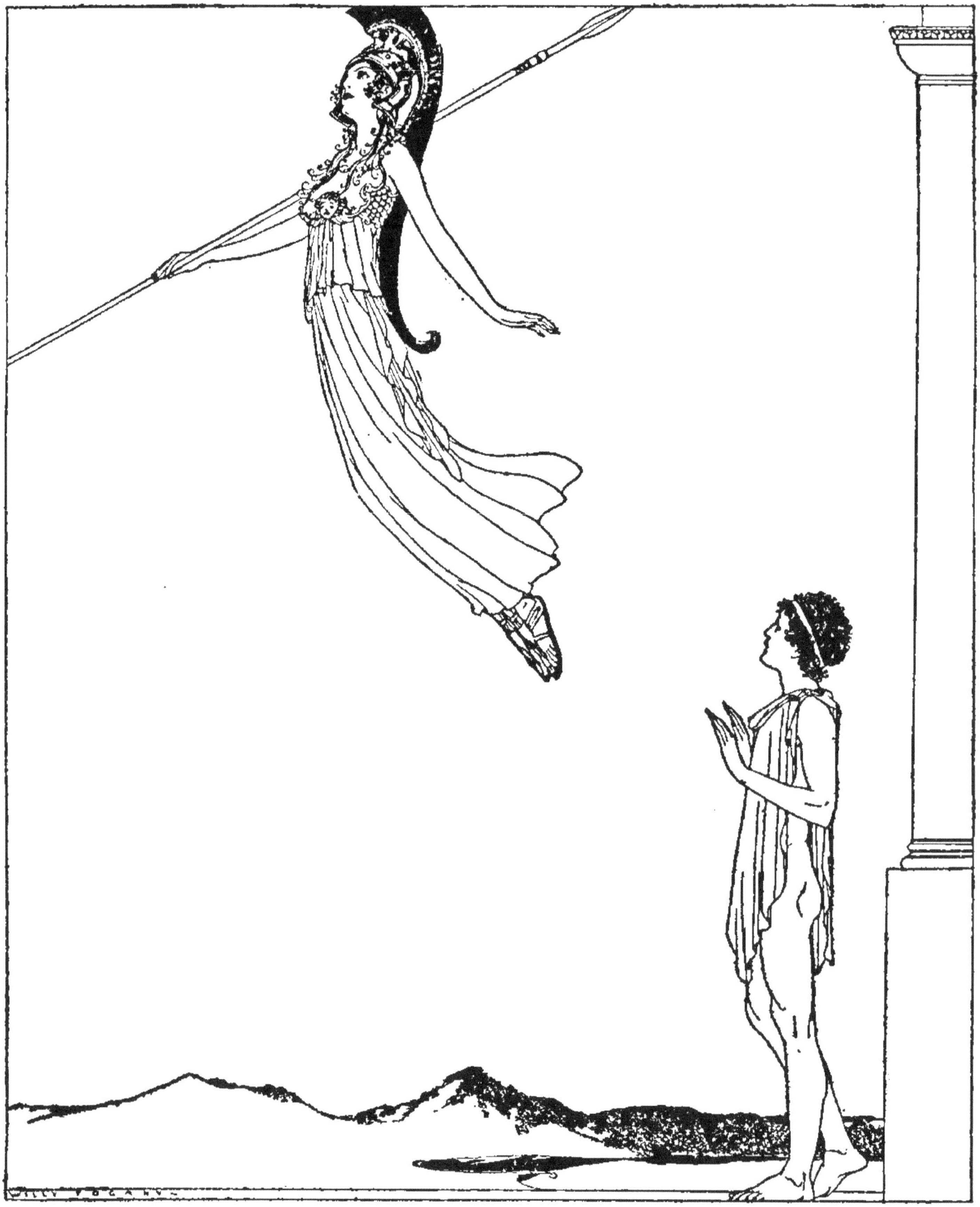
WILLY POGANY

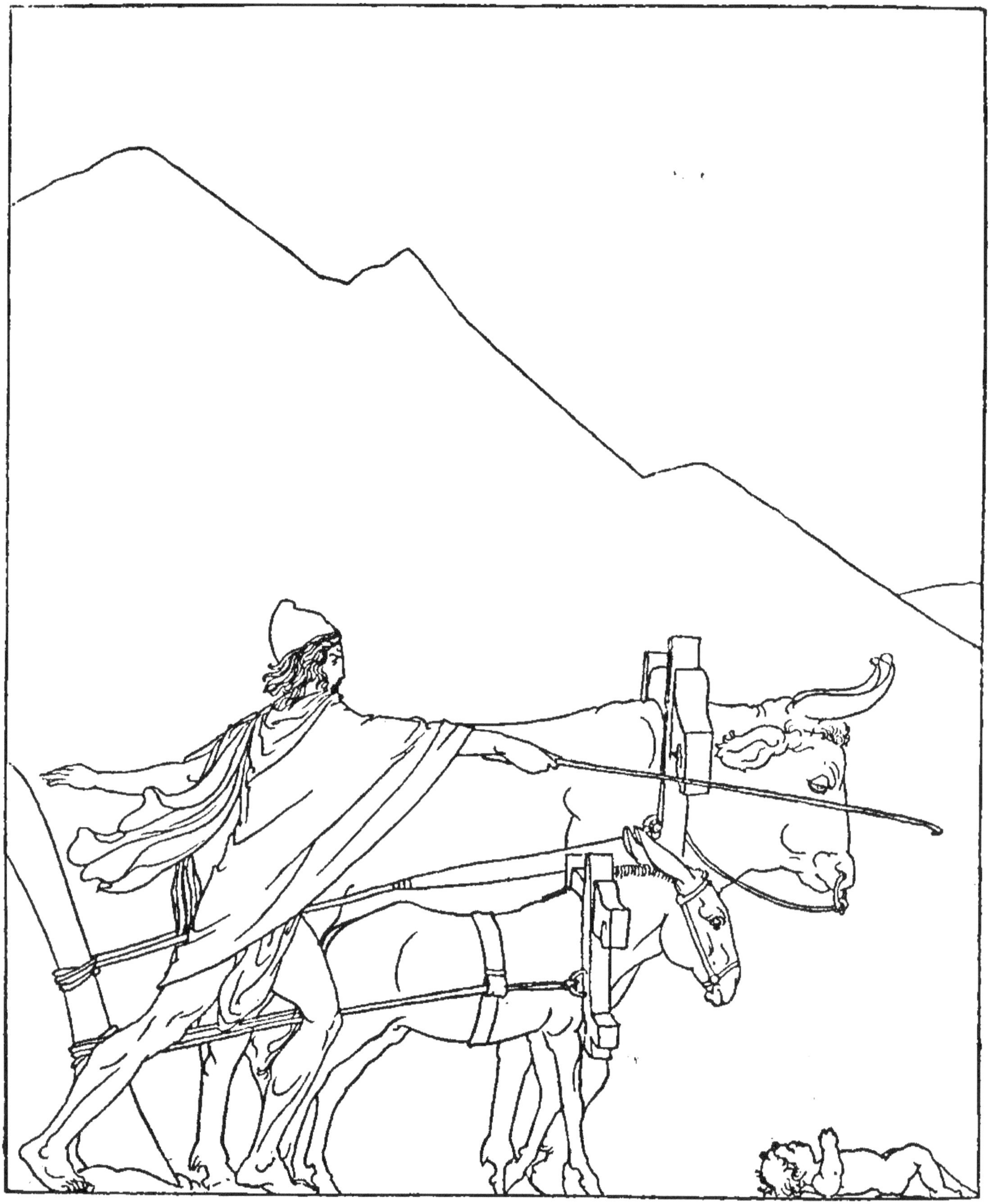

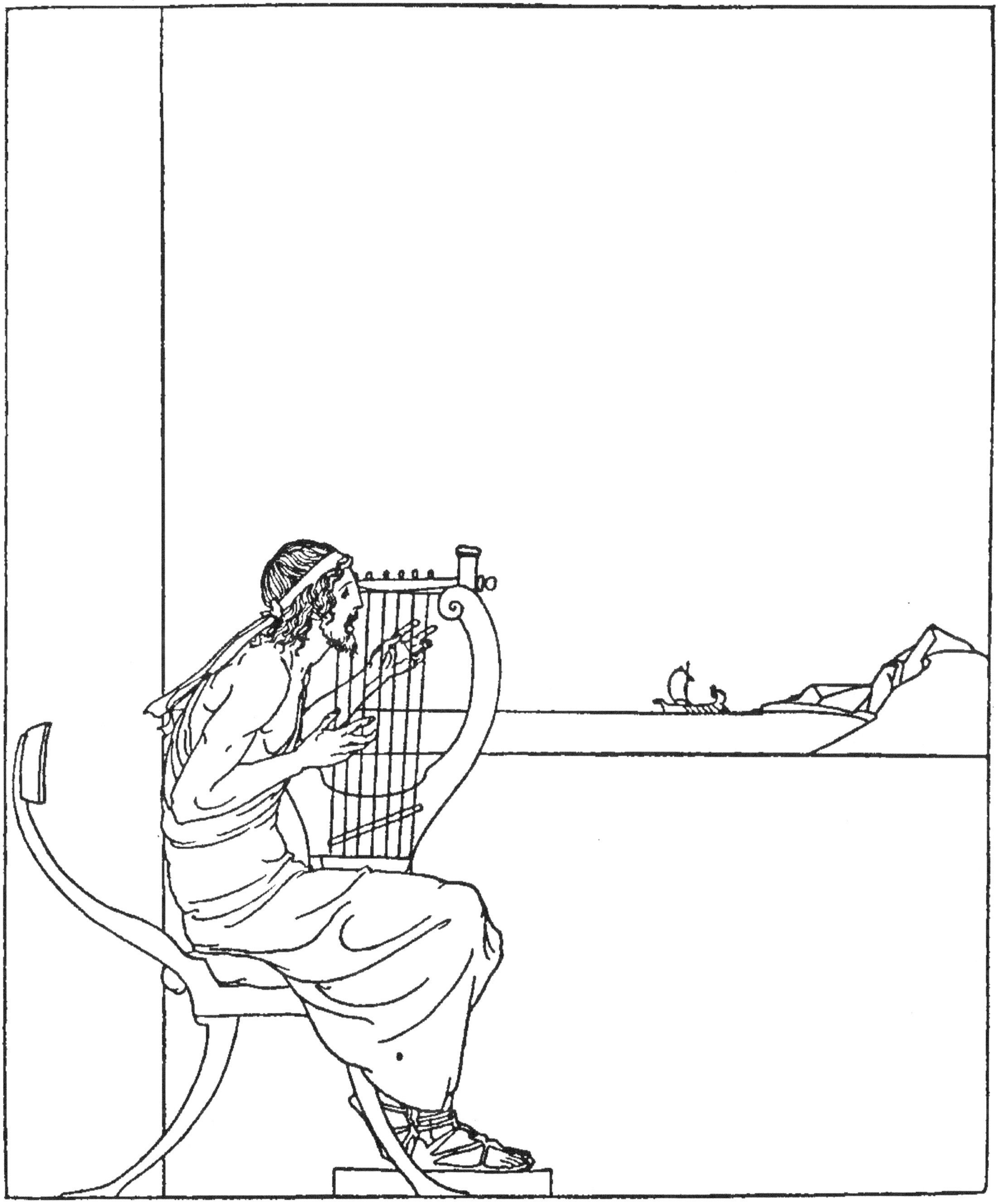

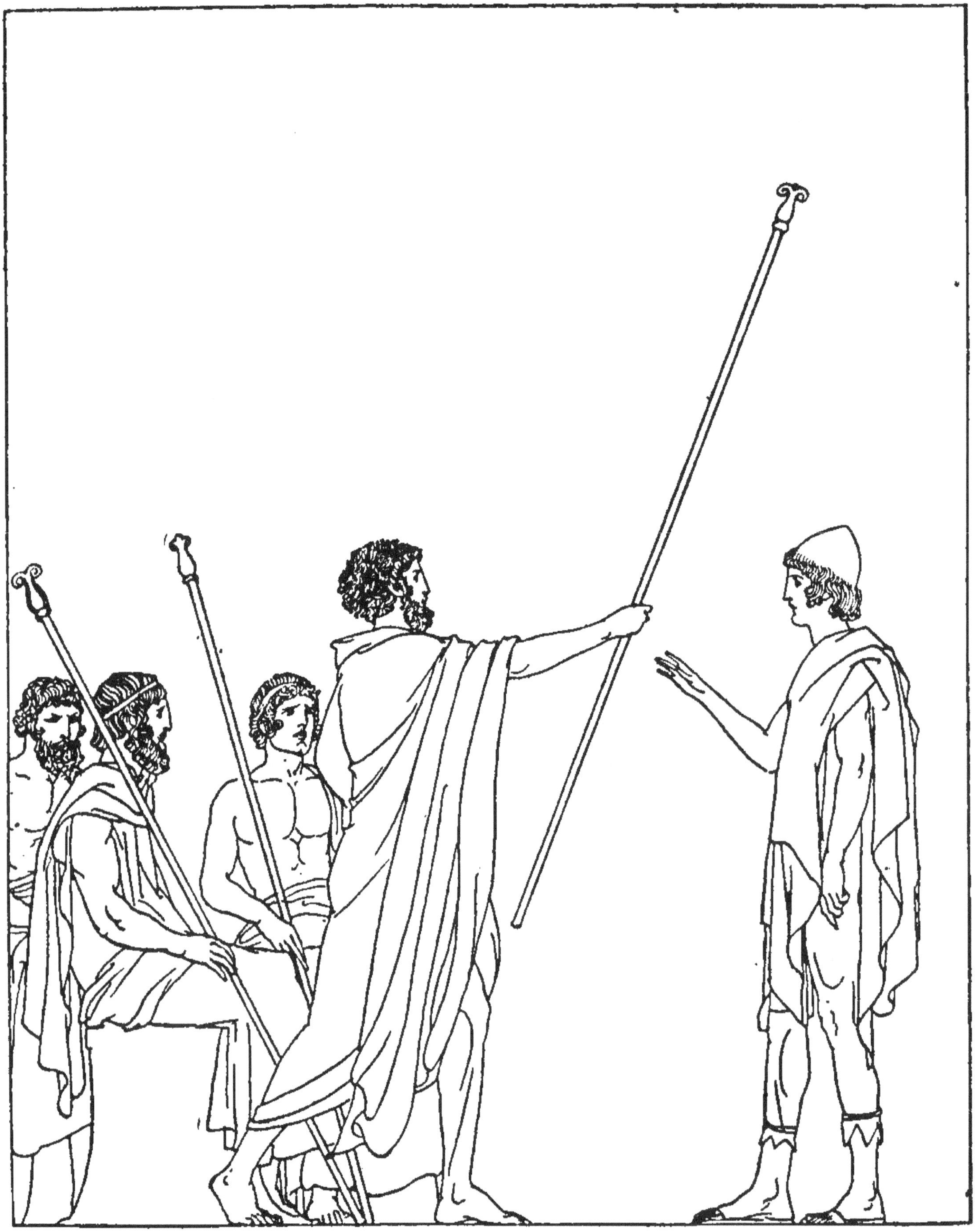

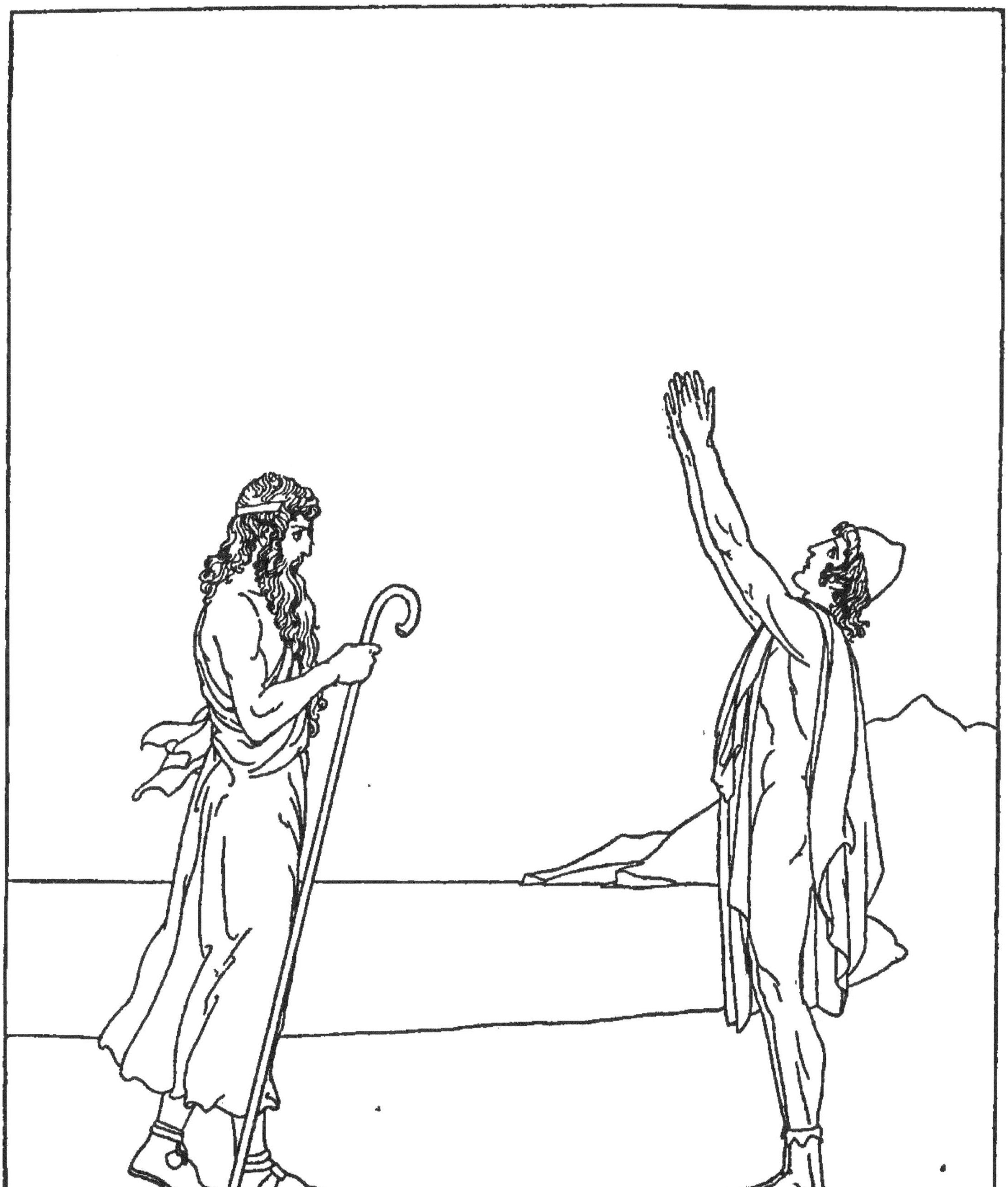

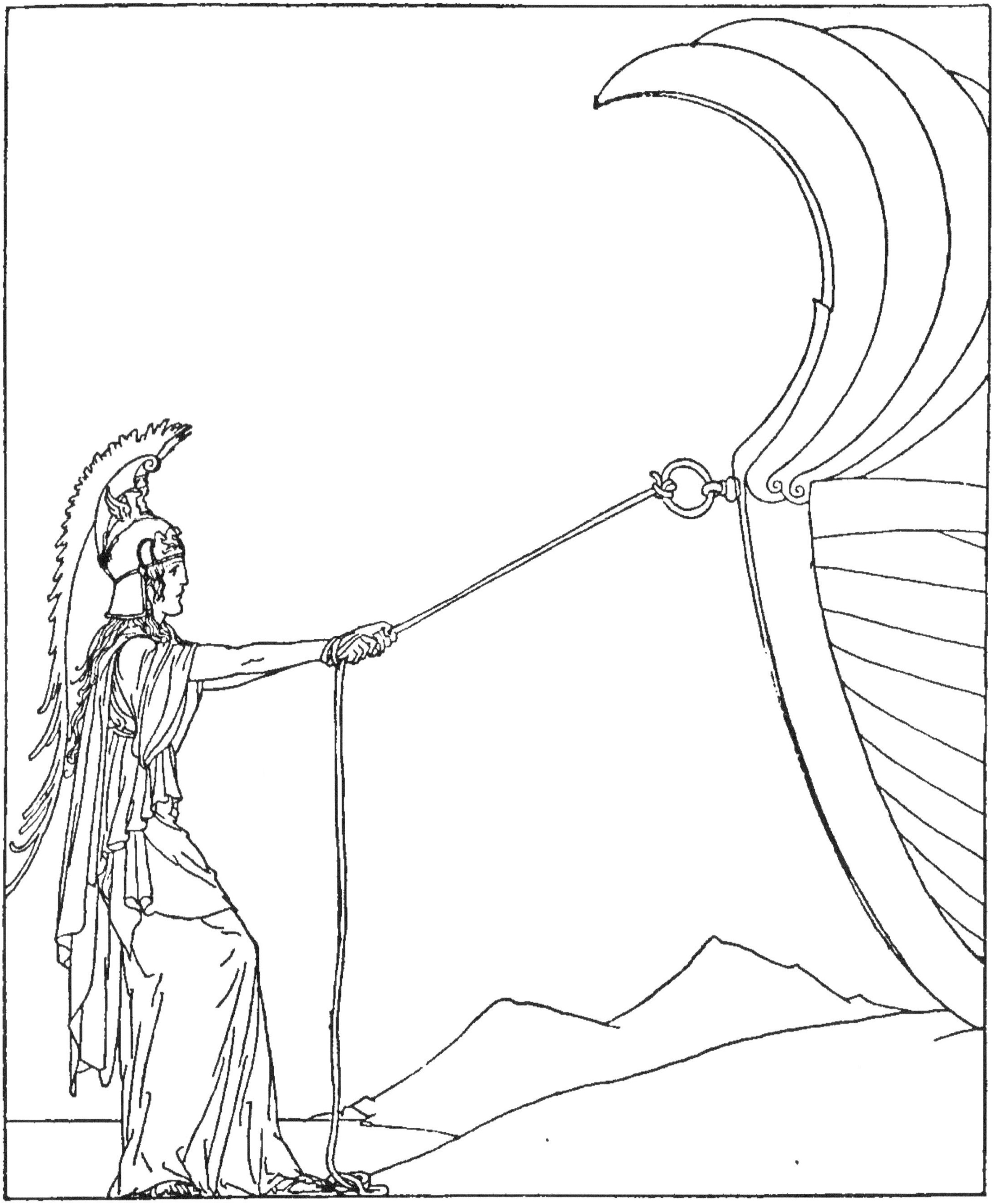

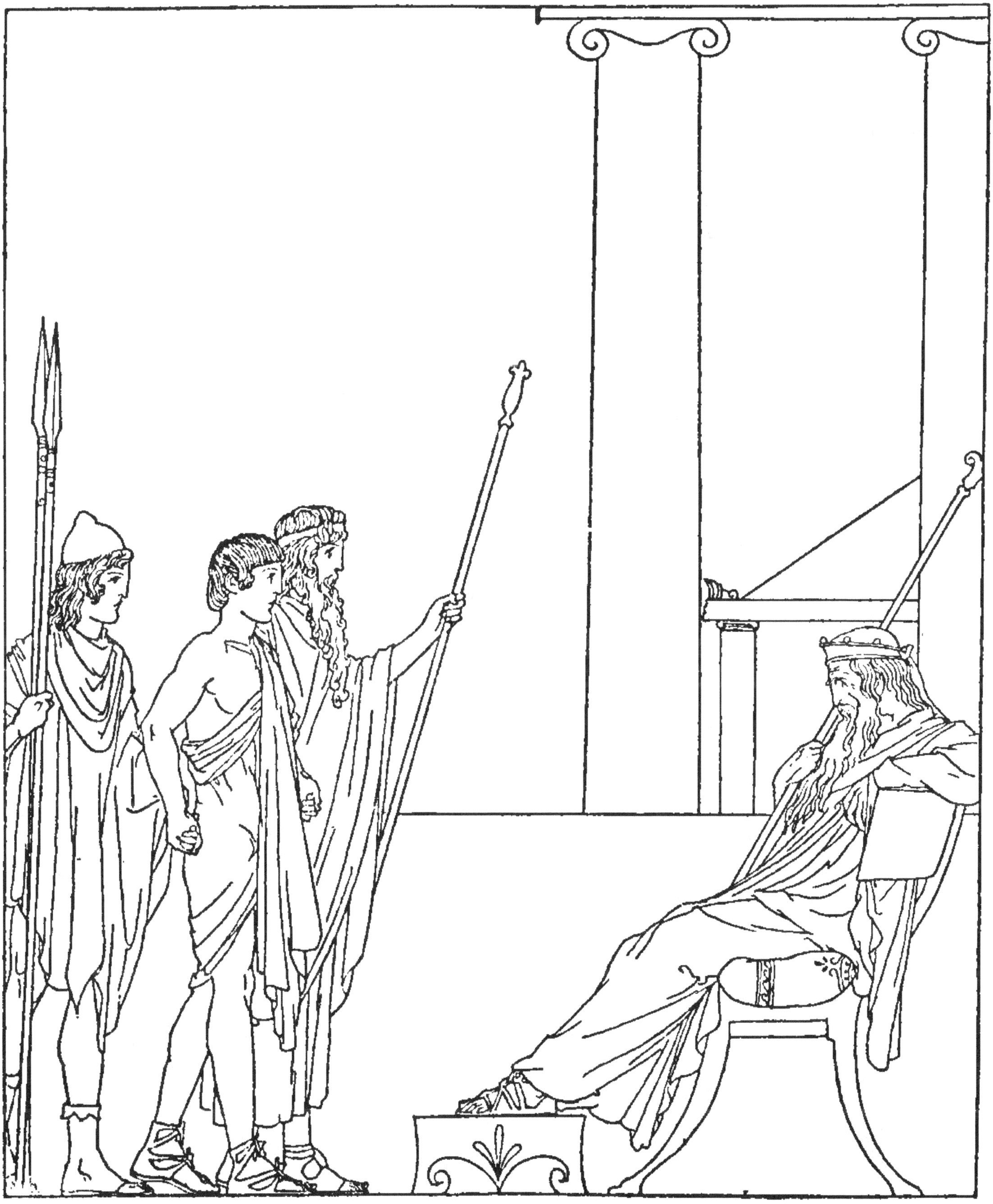

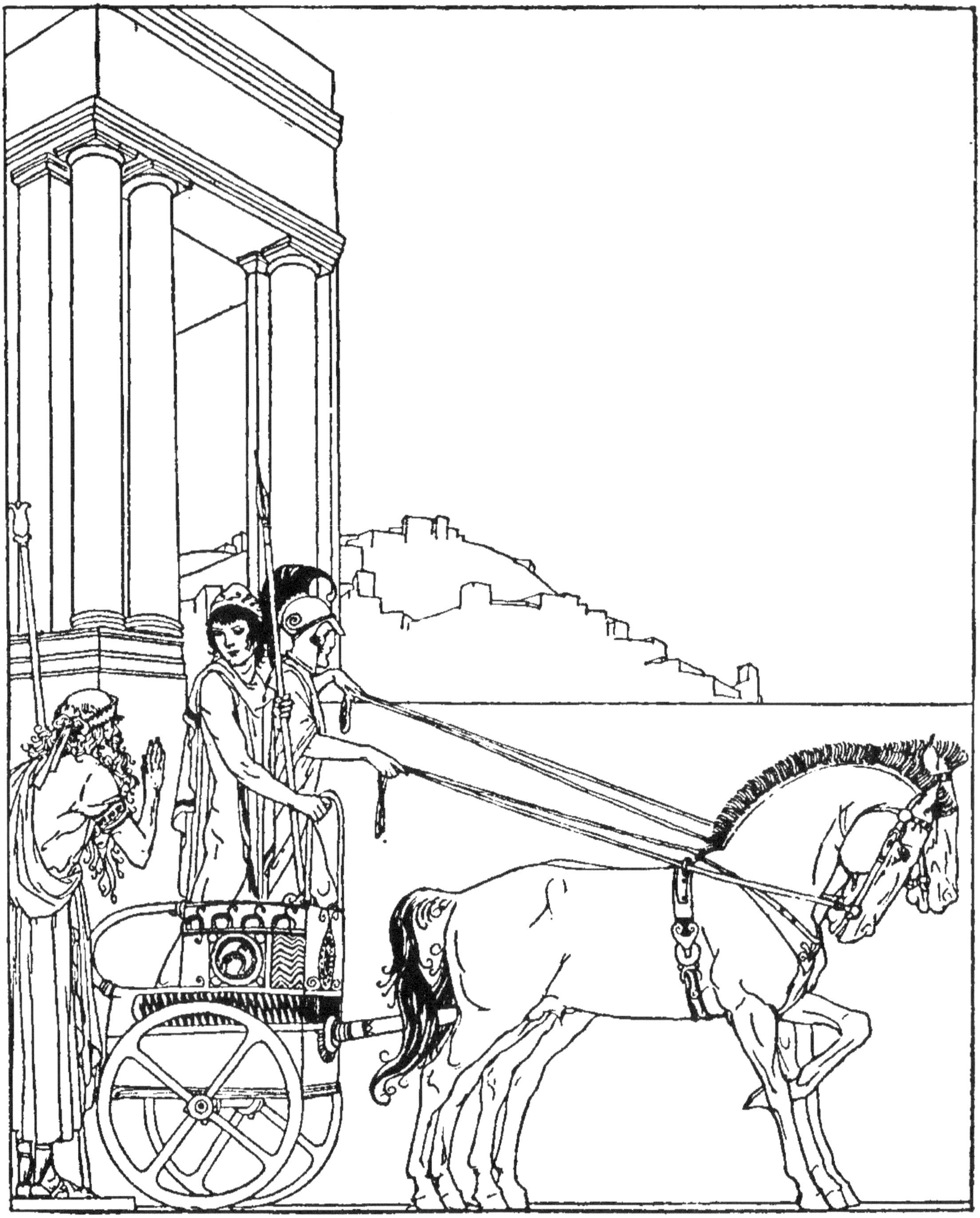

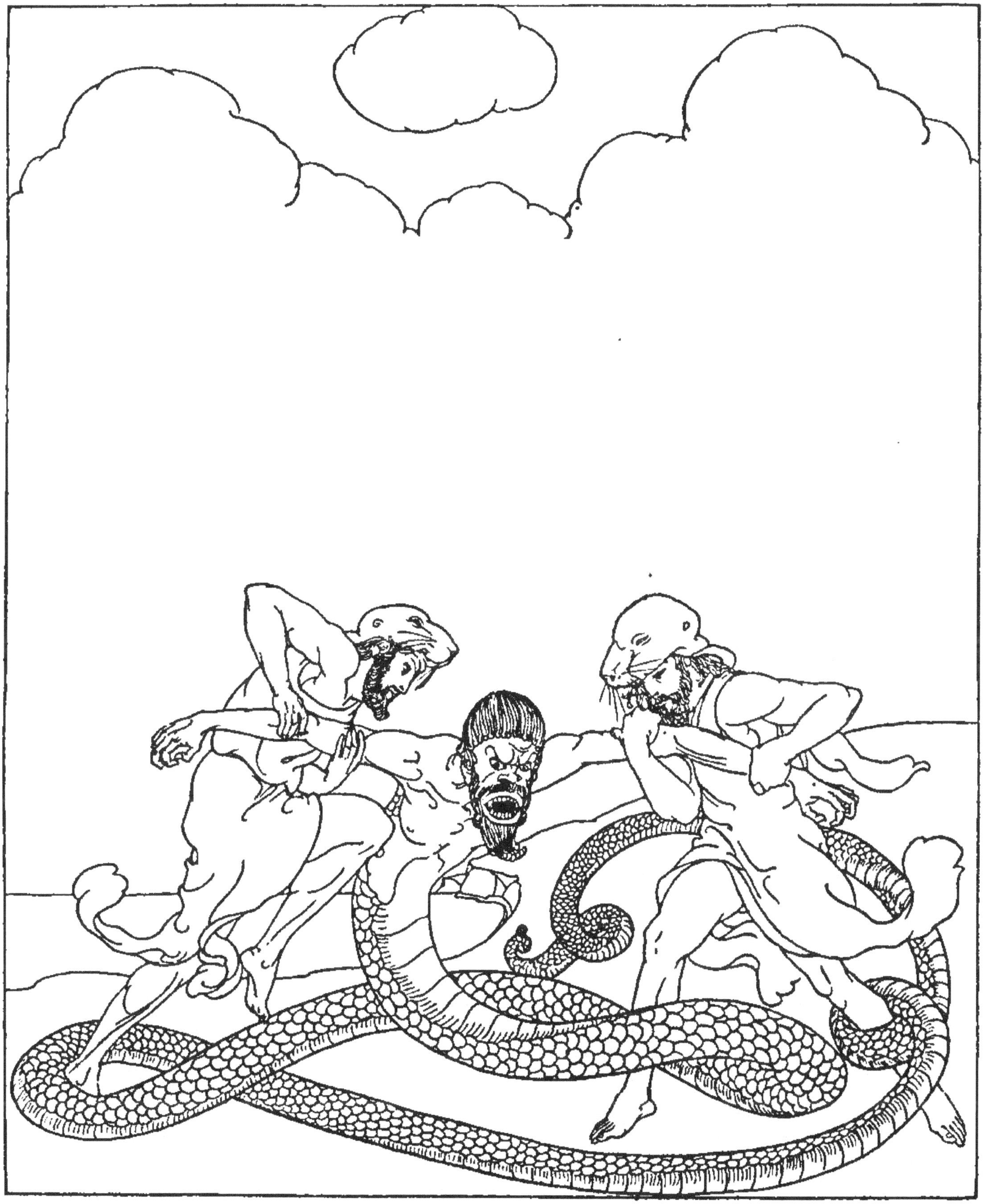

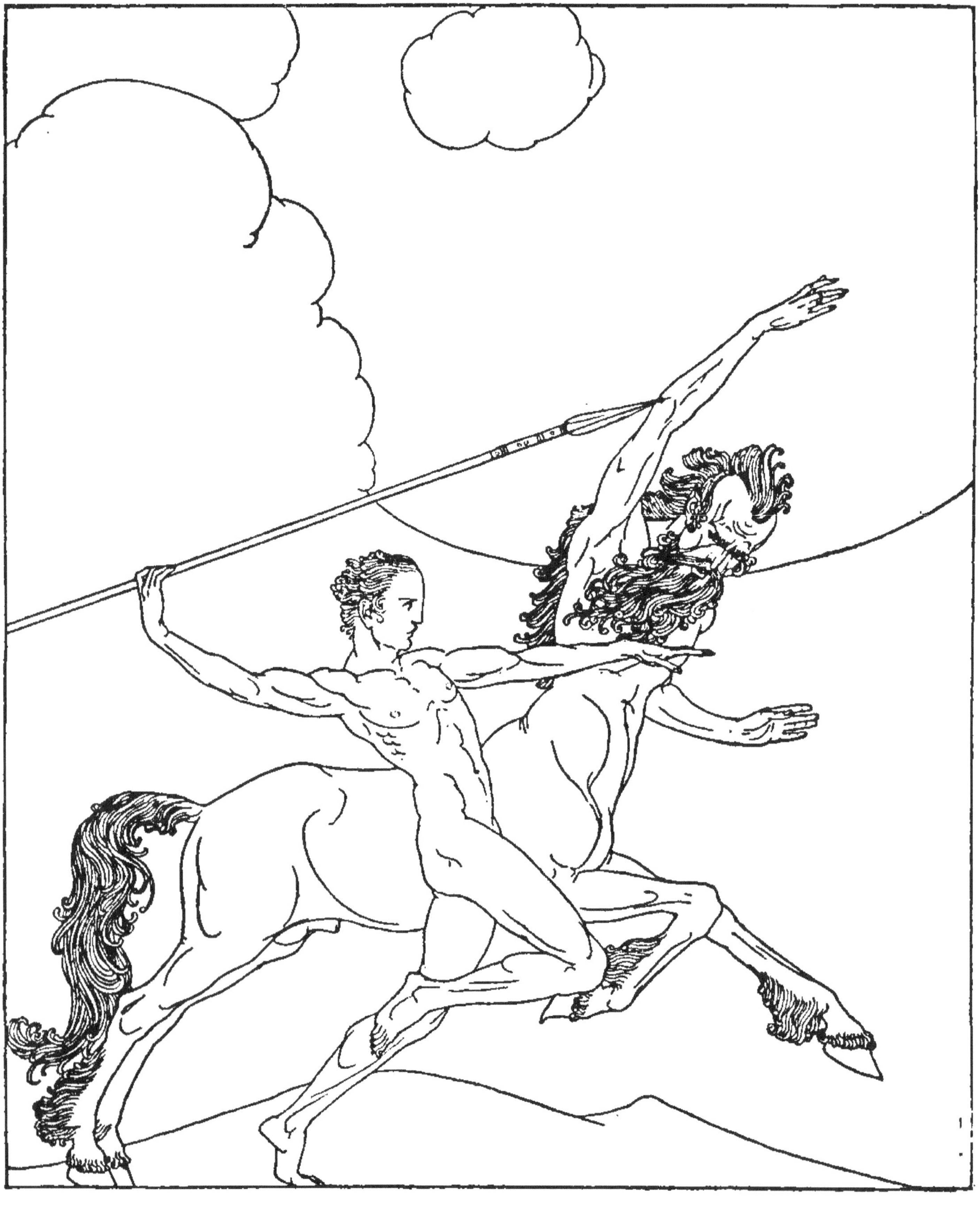

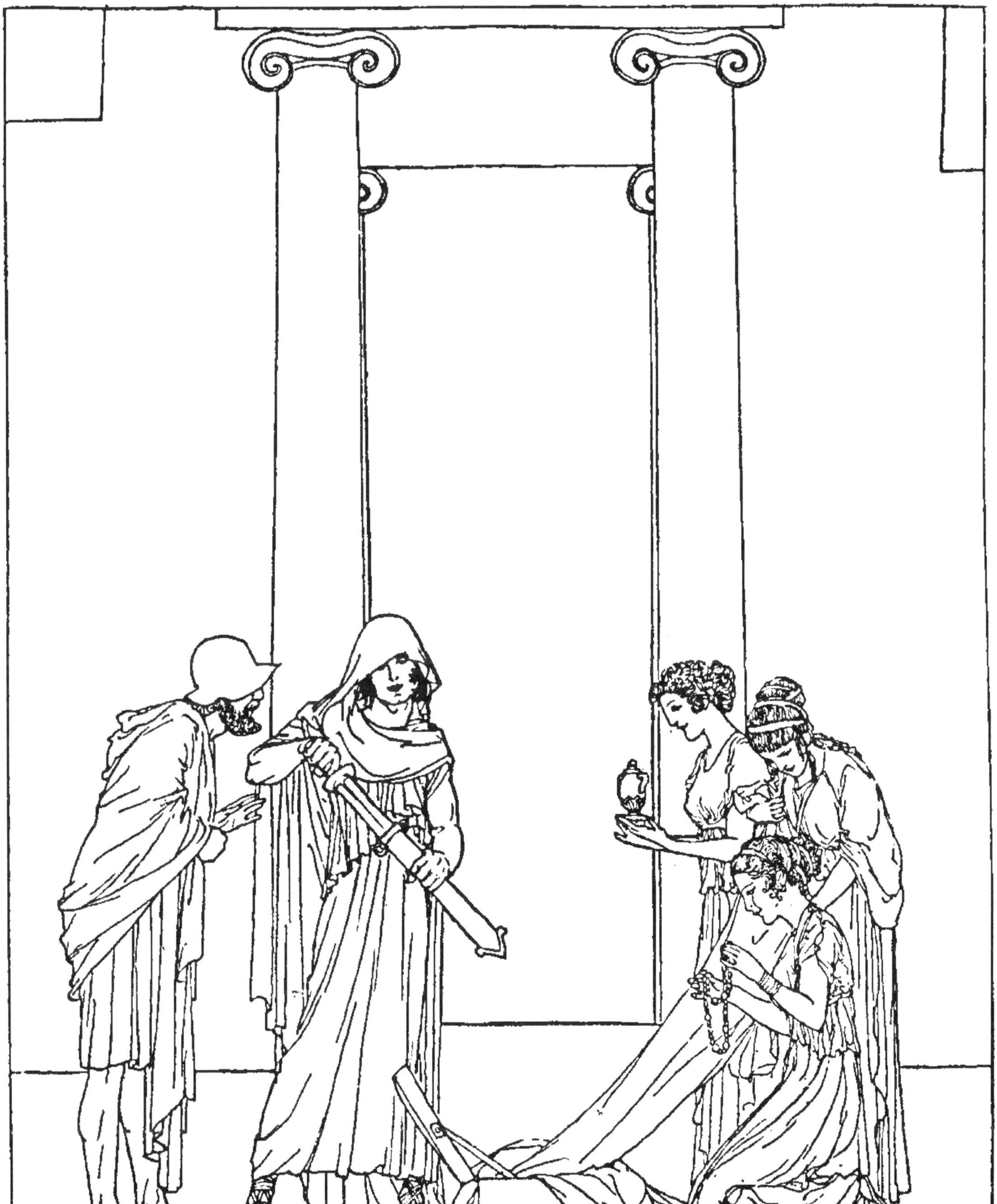

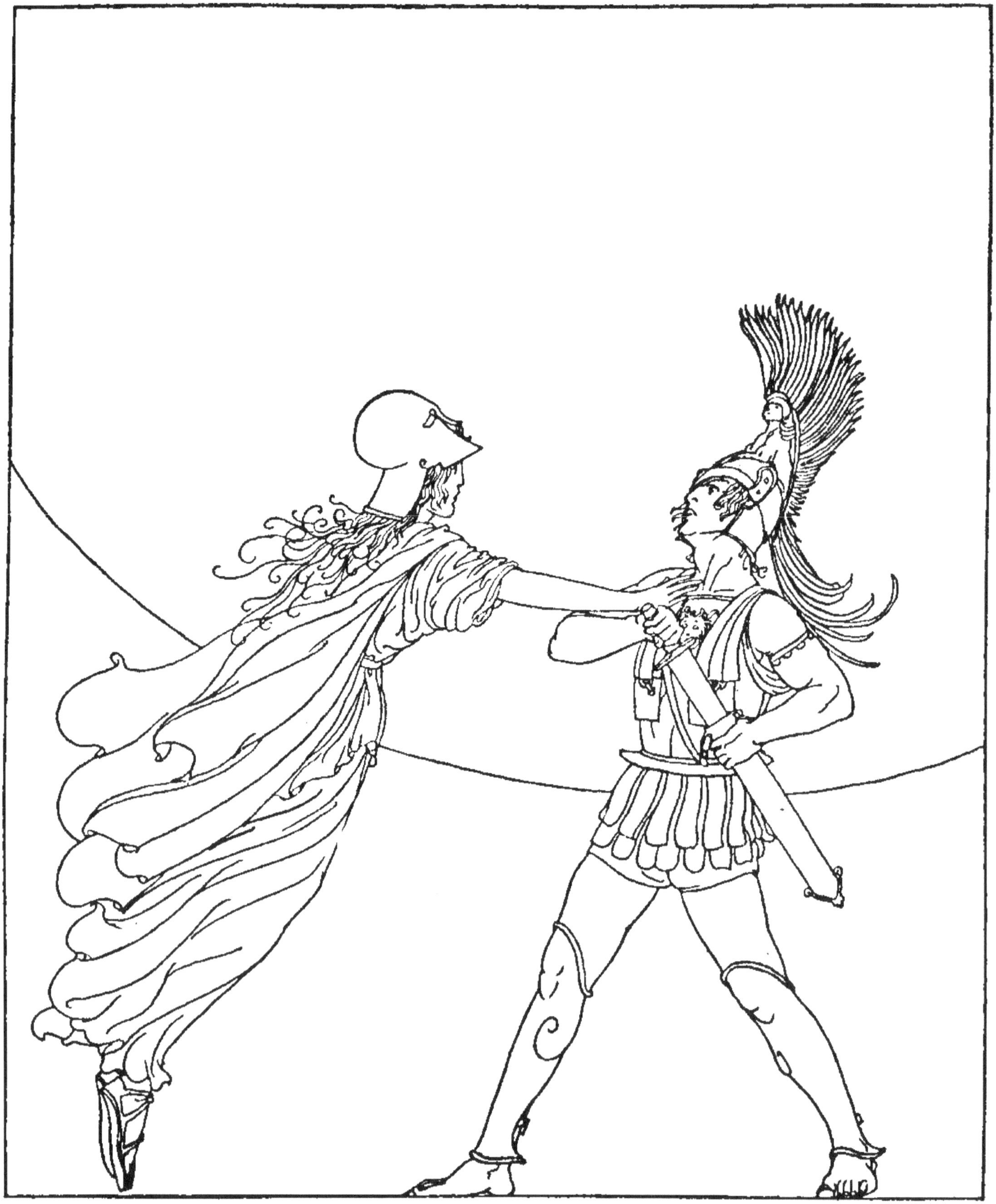

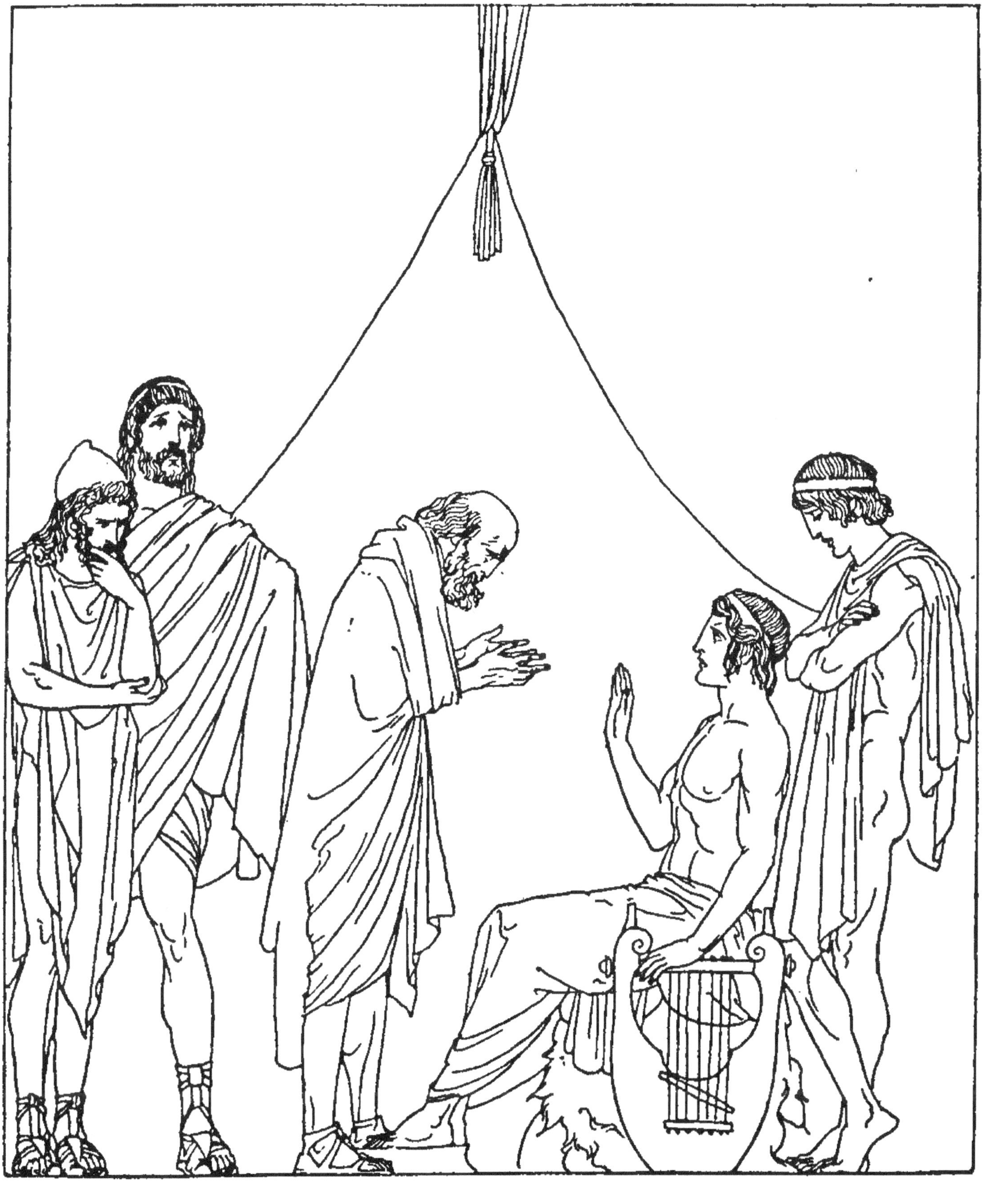

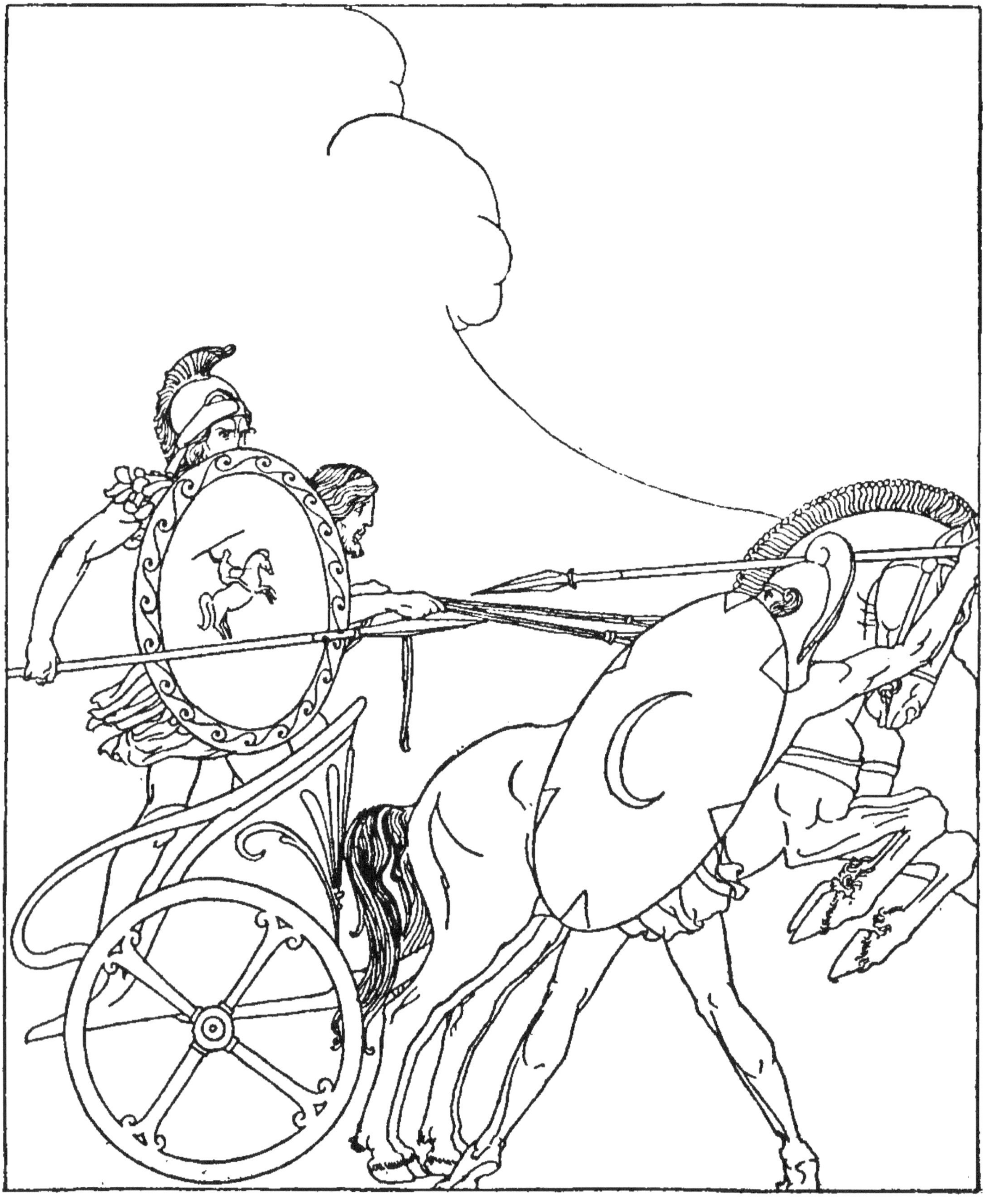

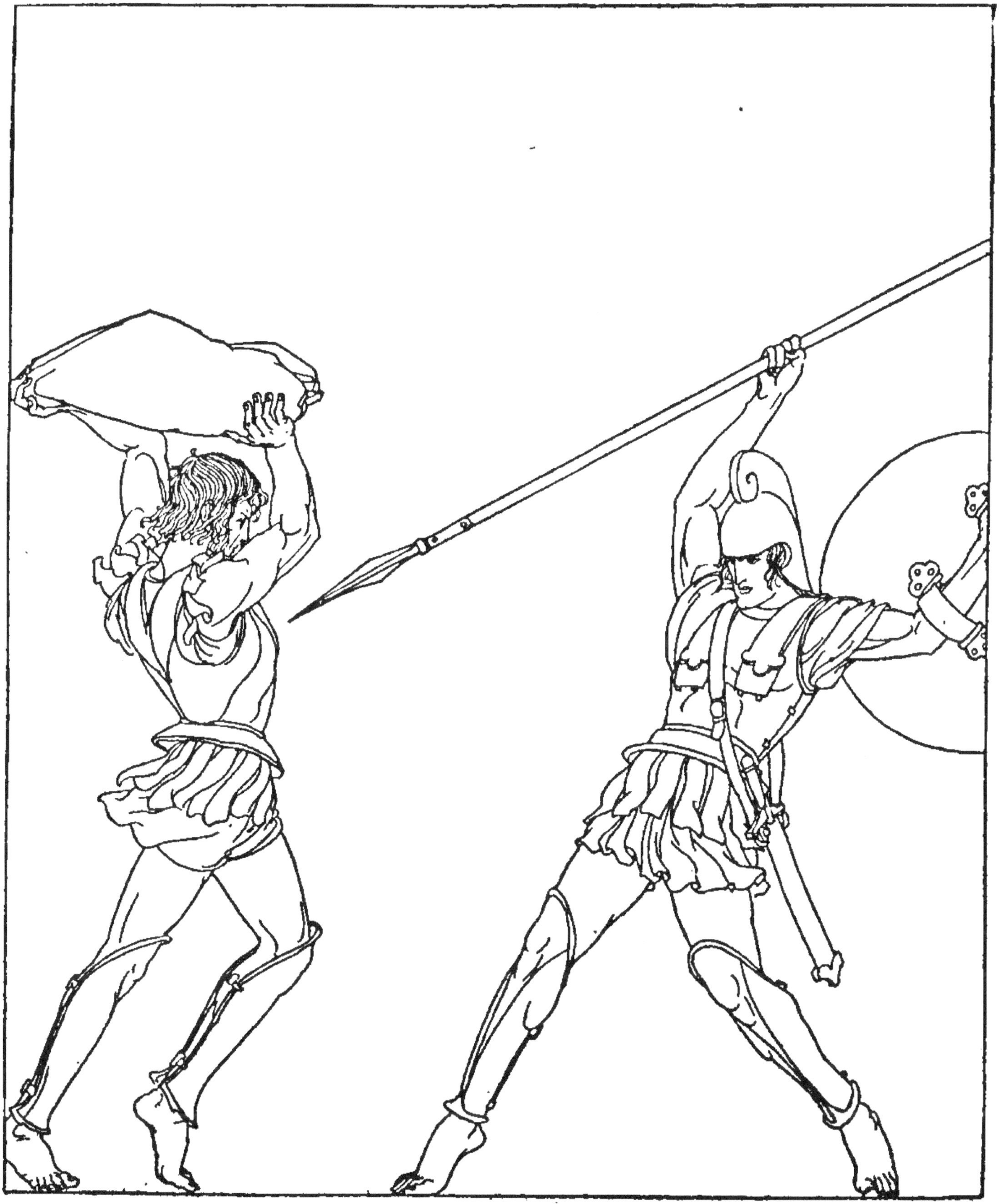

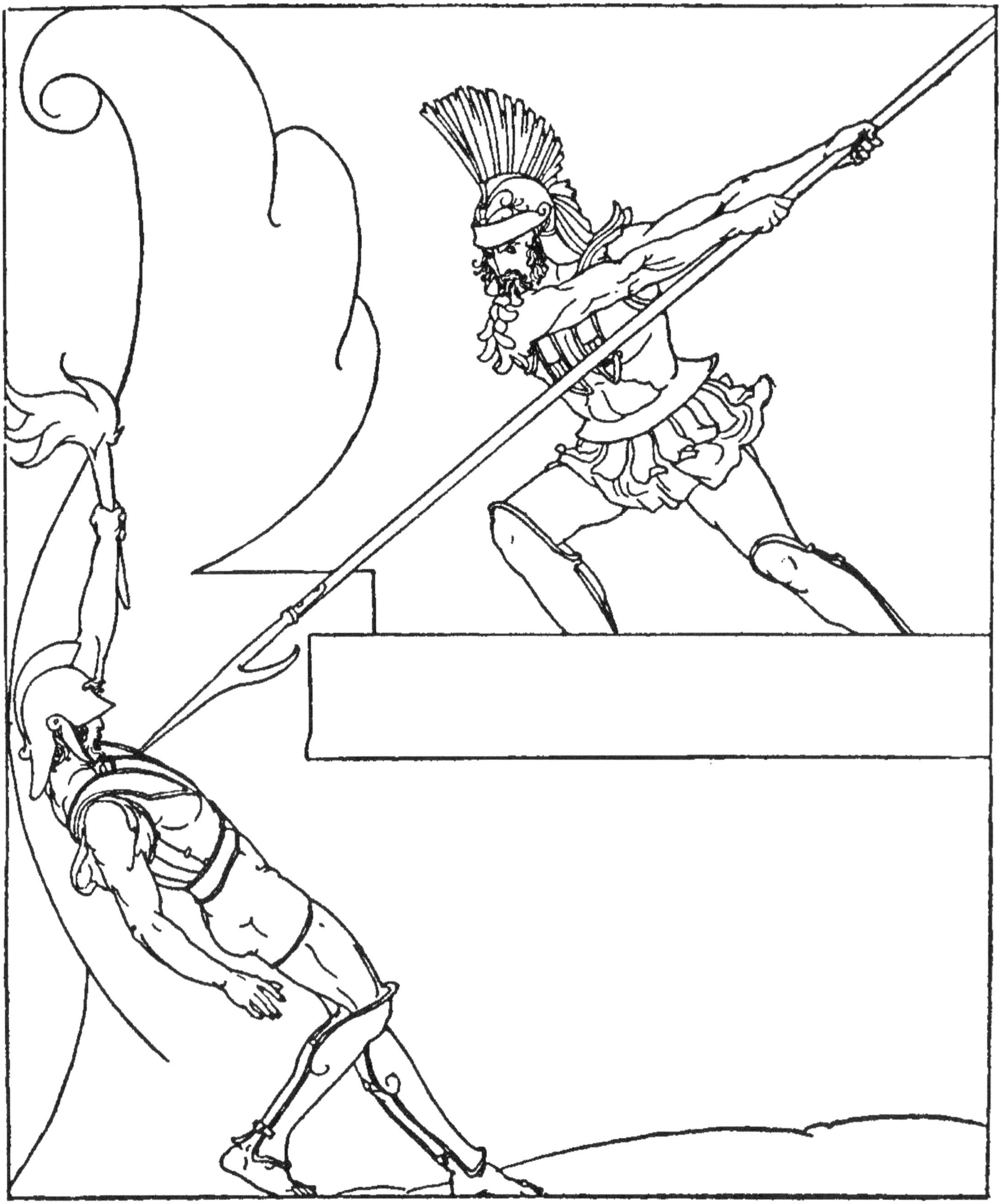

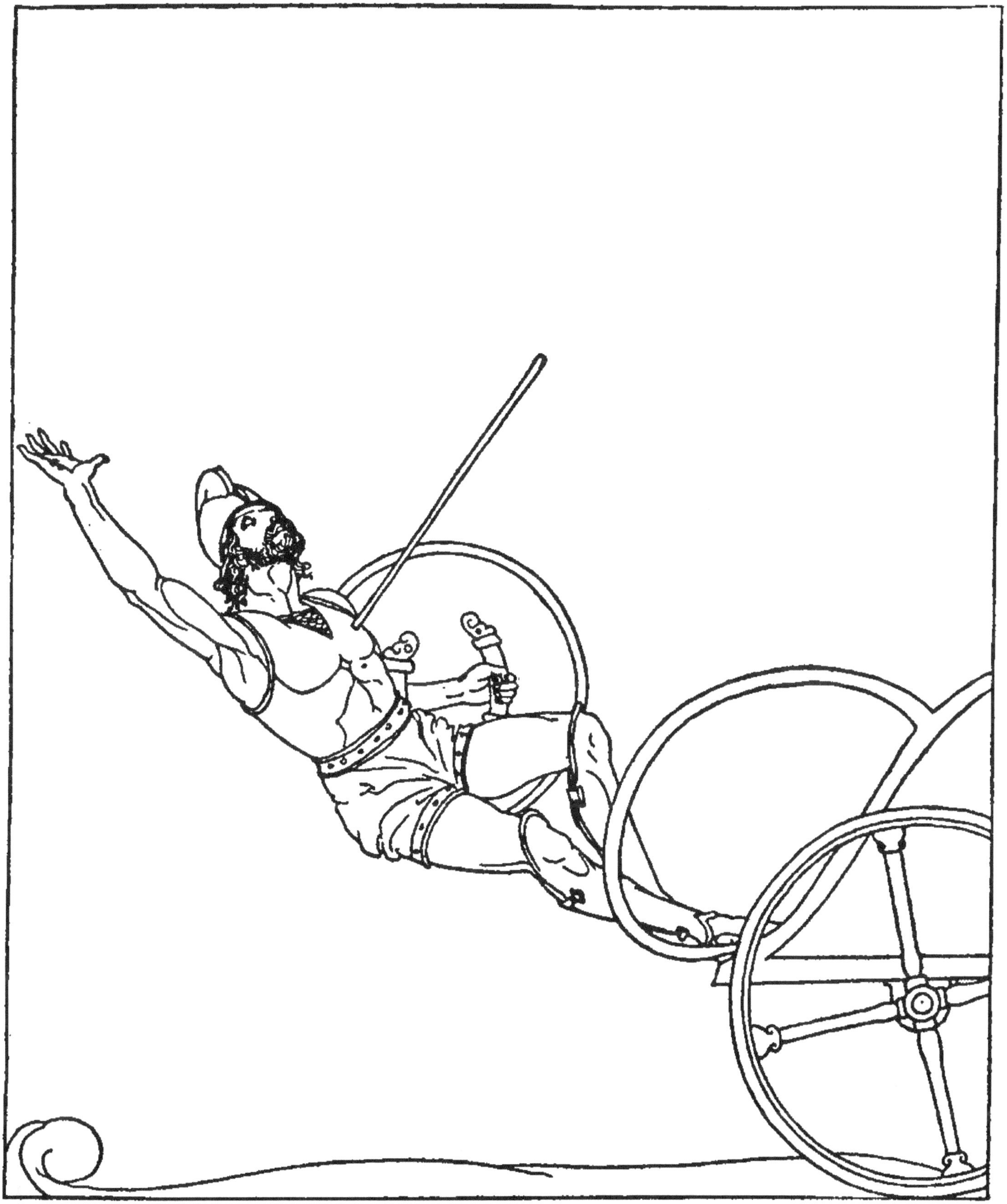

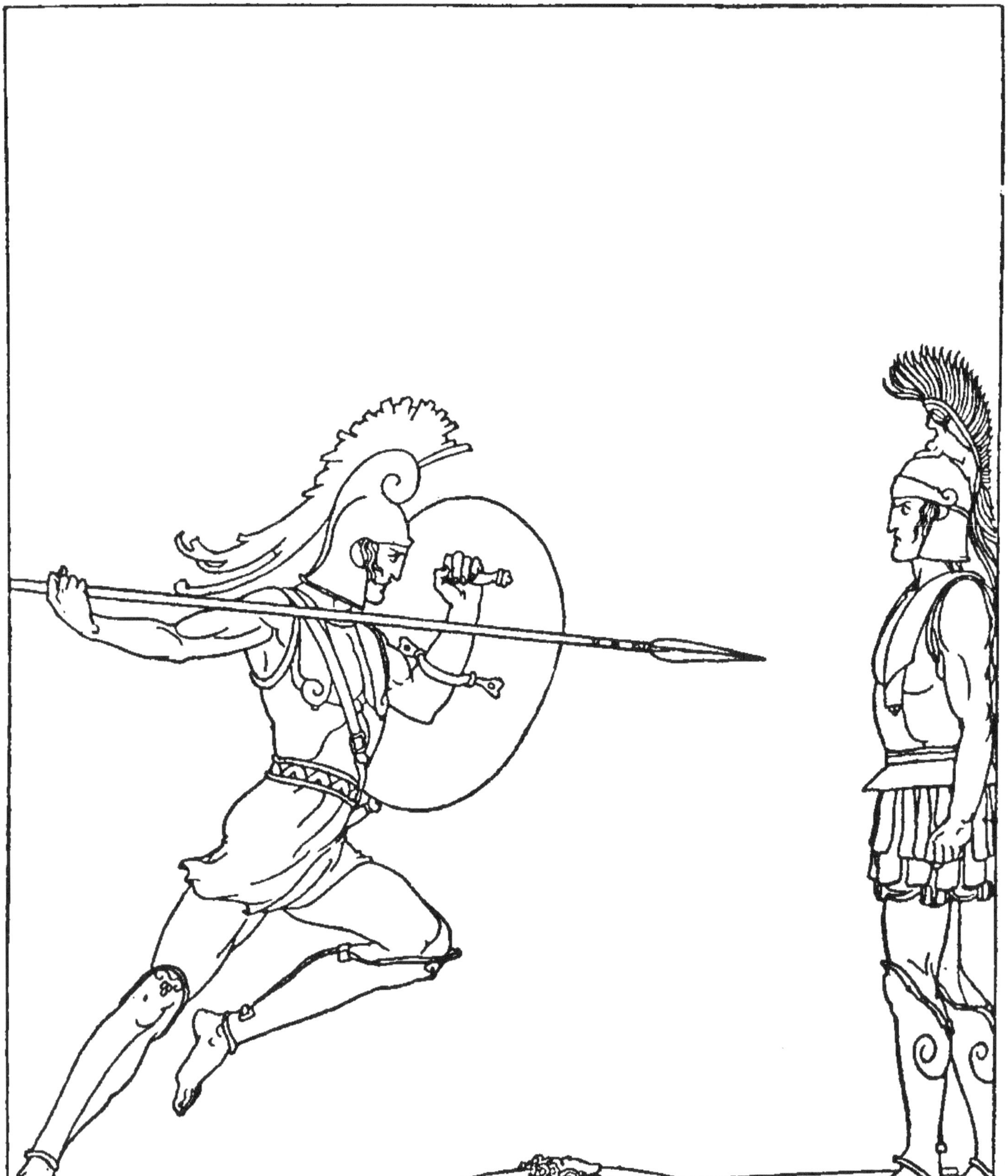

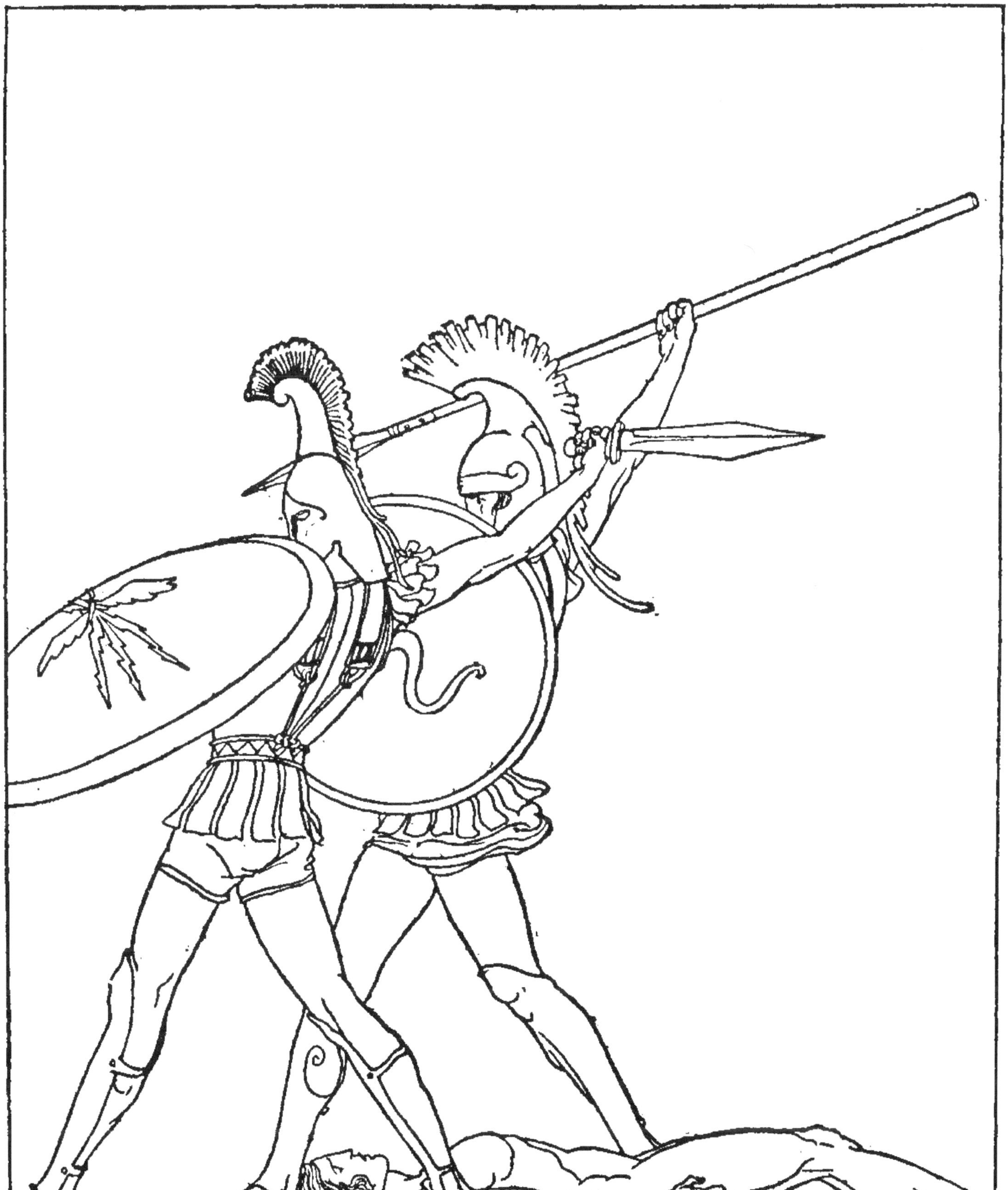

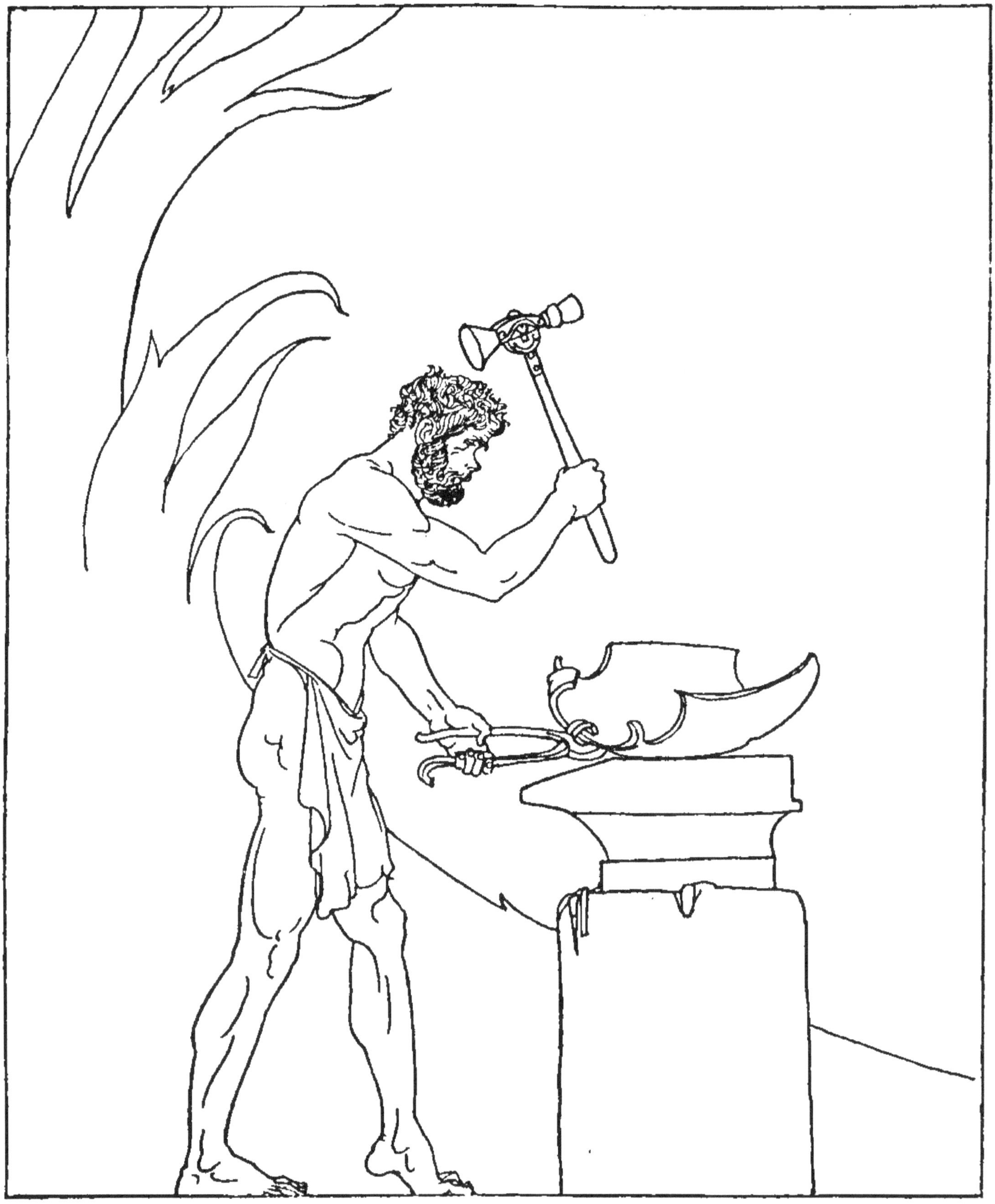

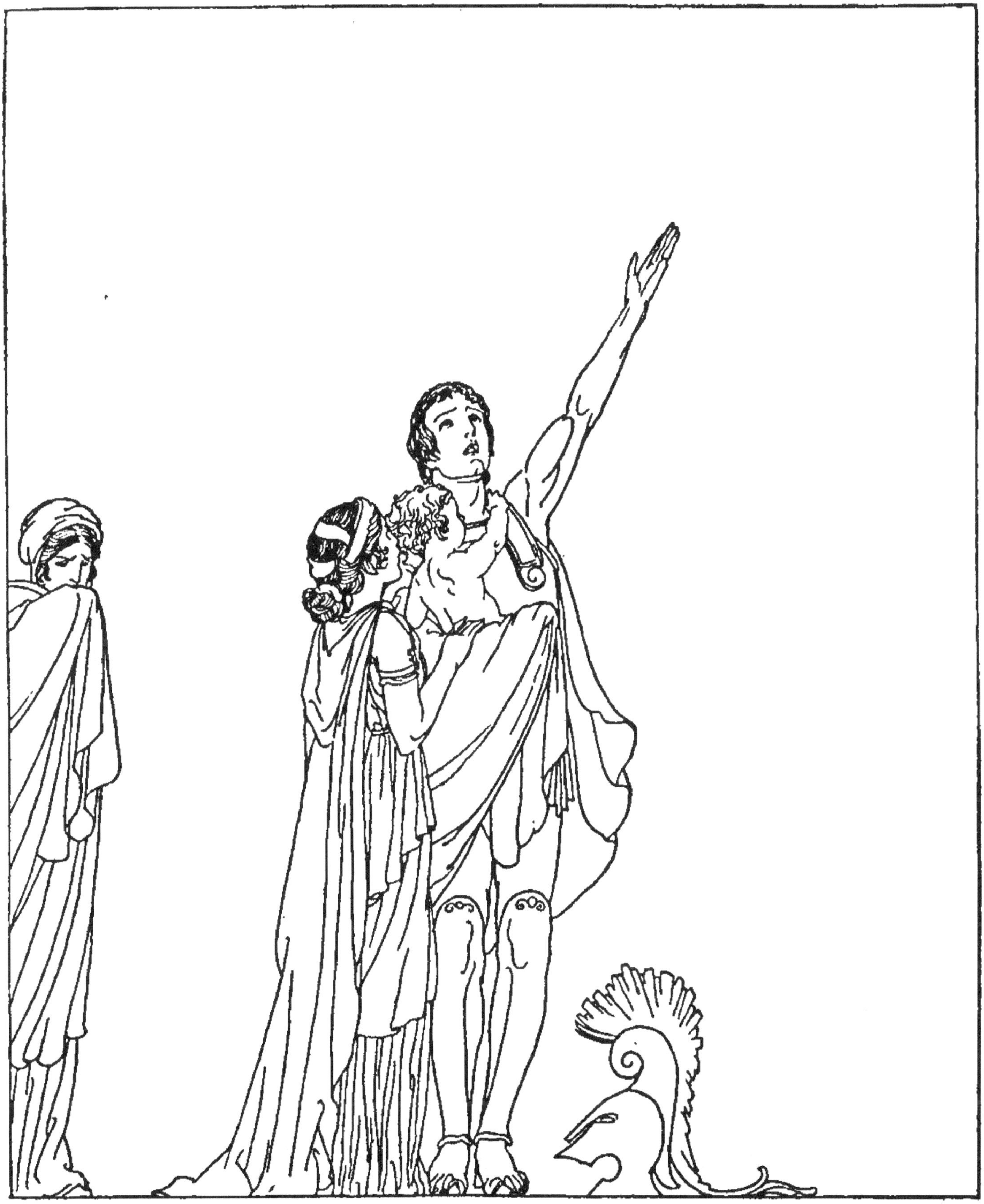

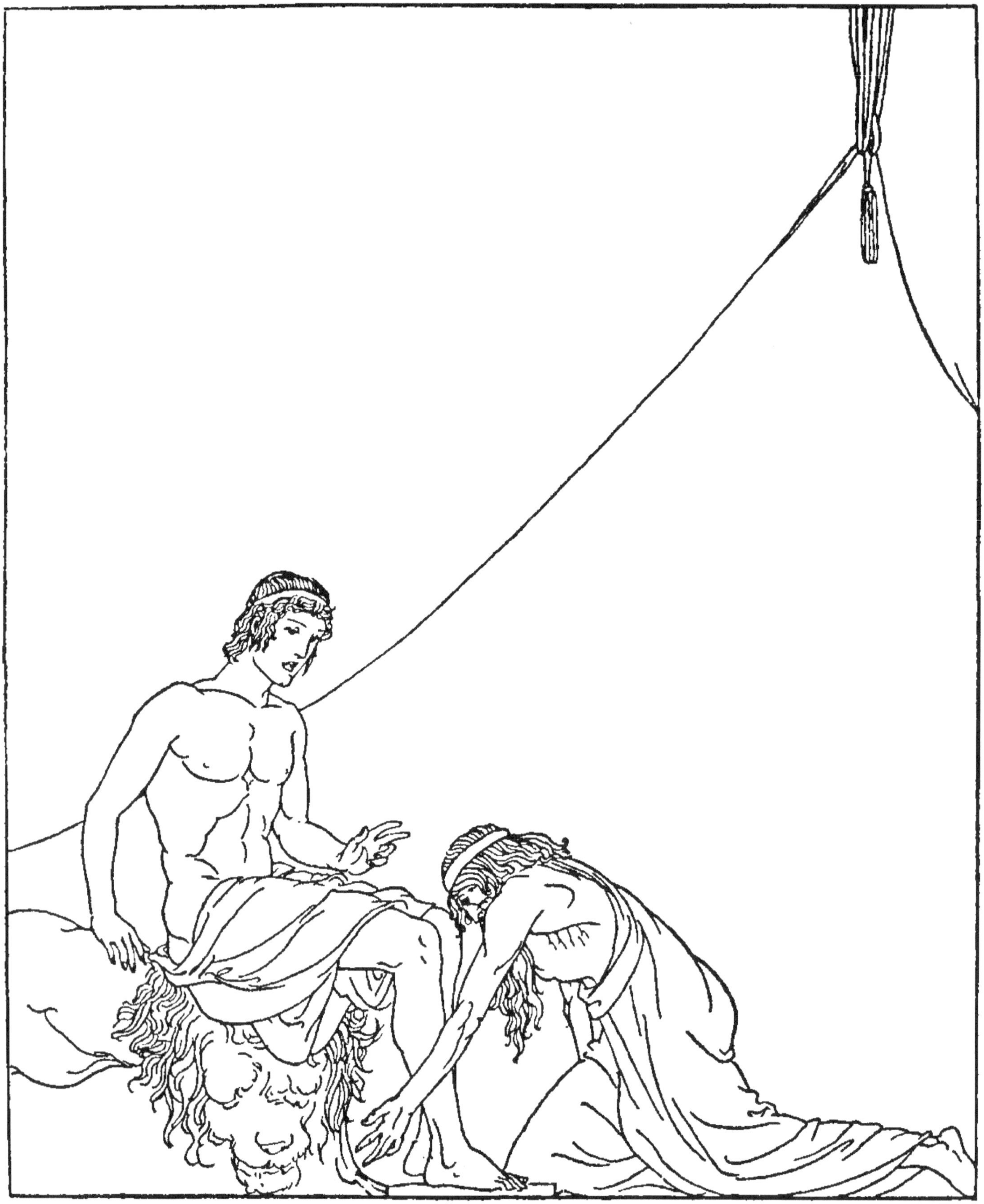

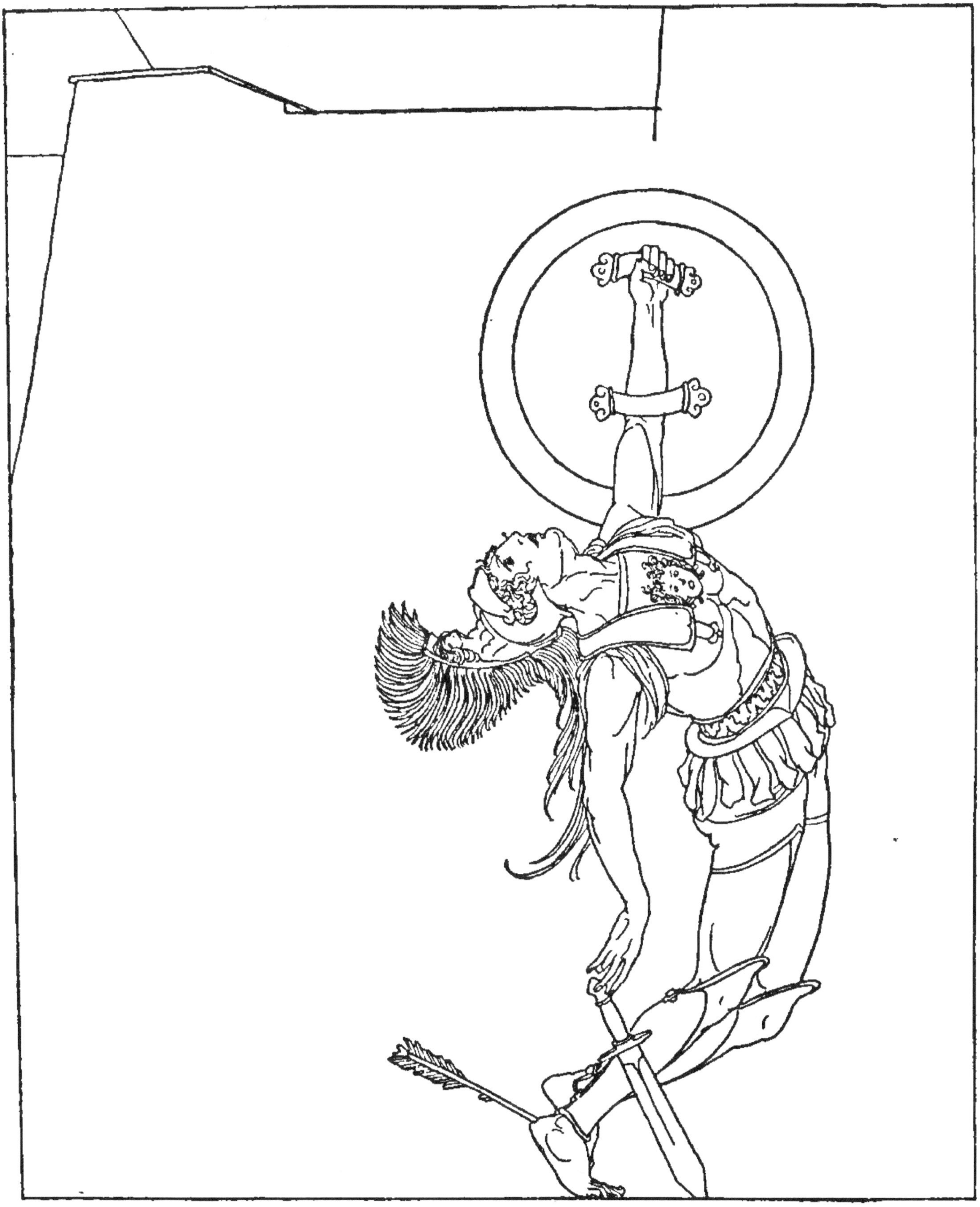

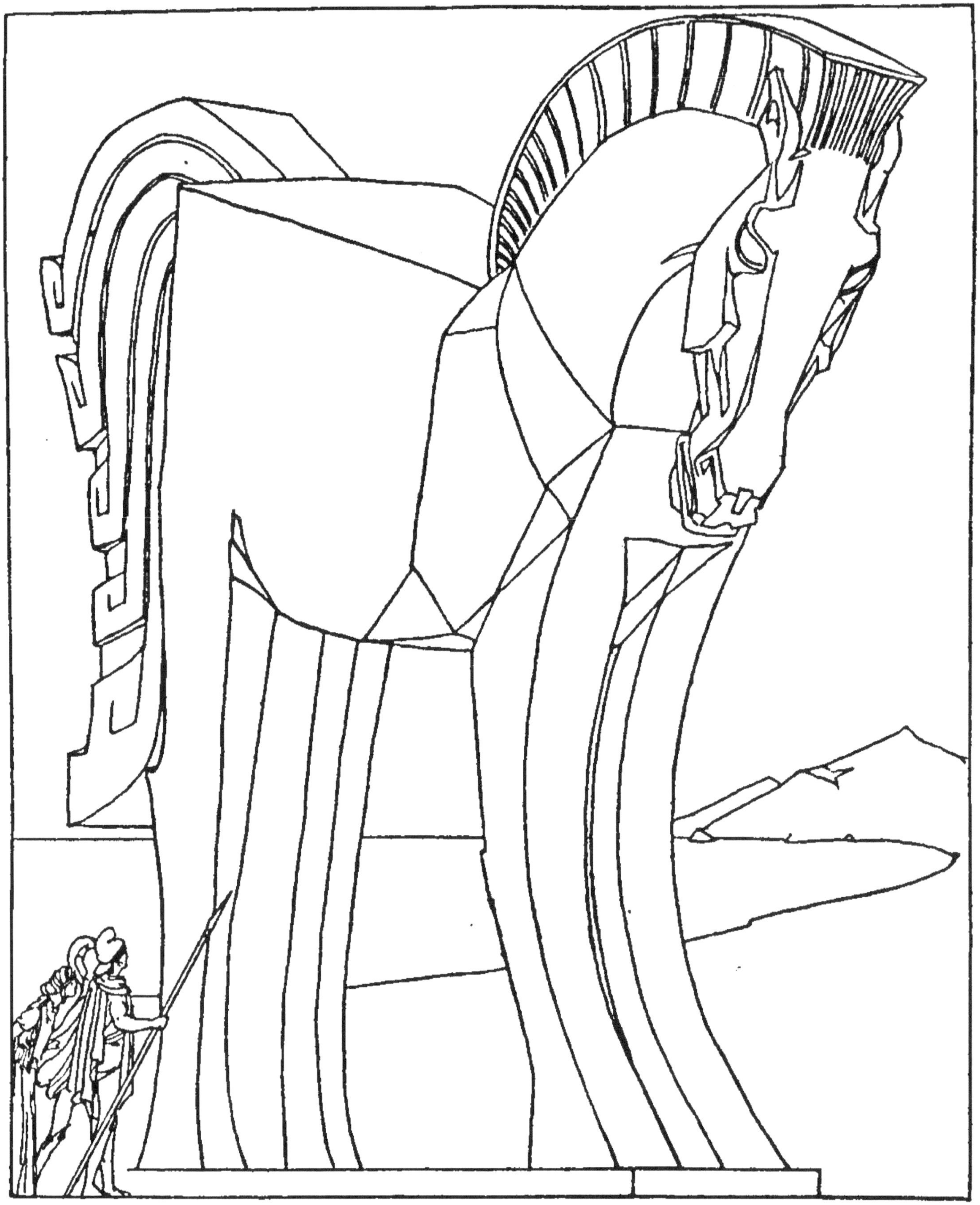

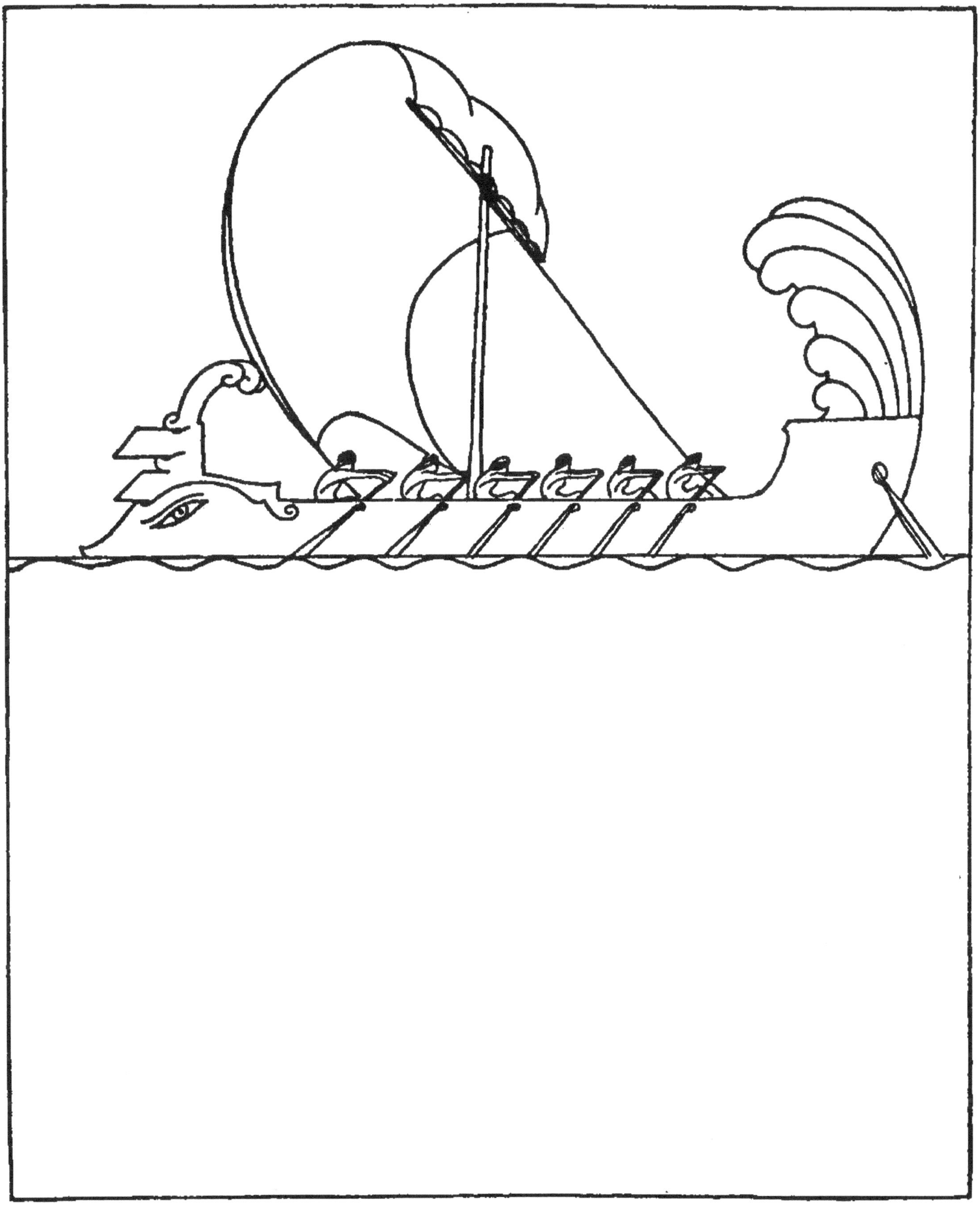

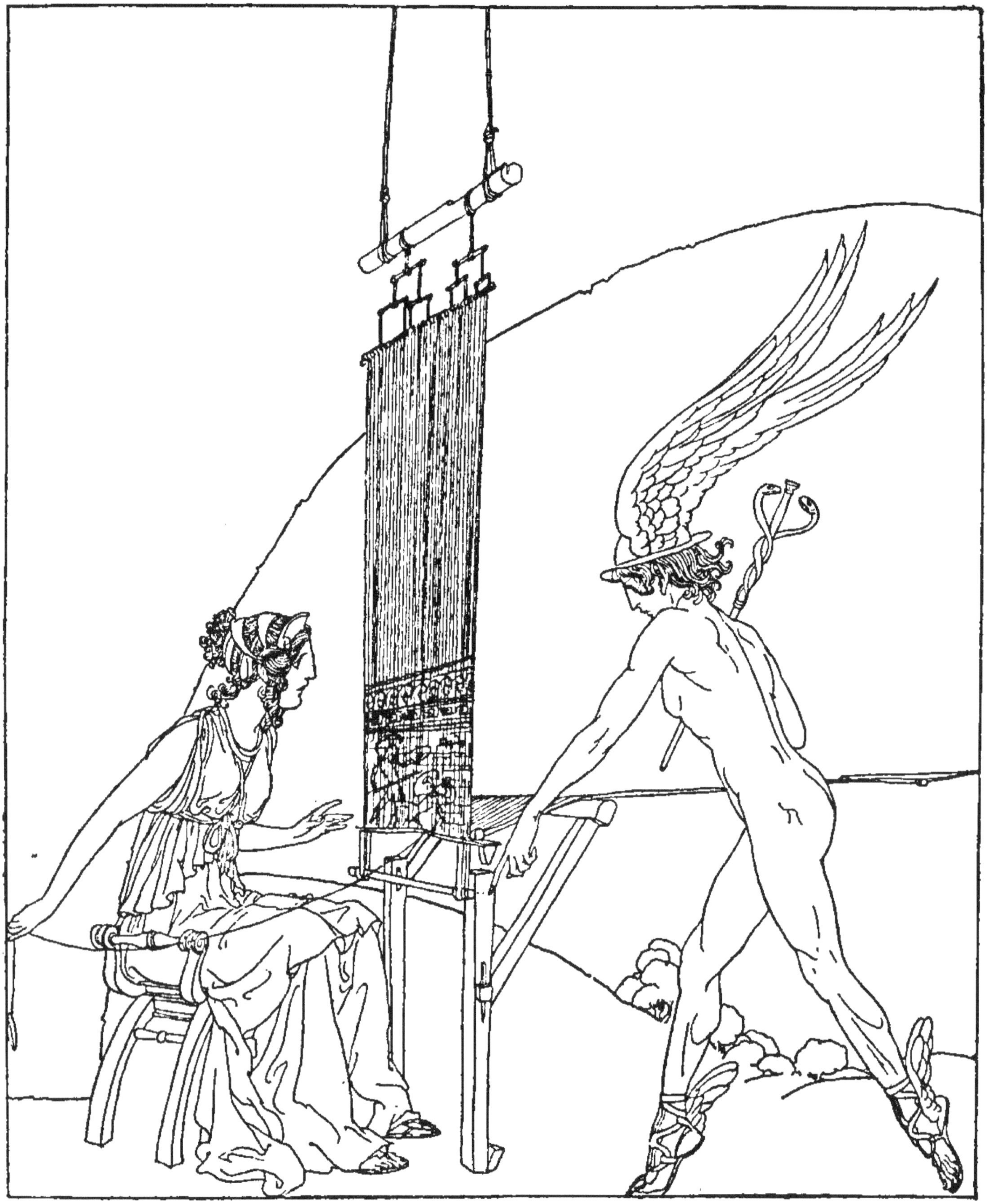

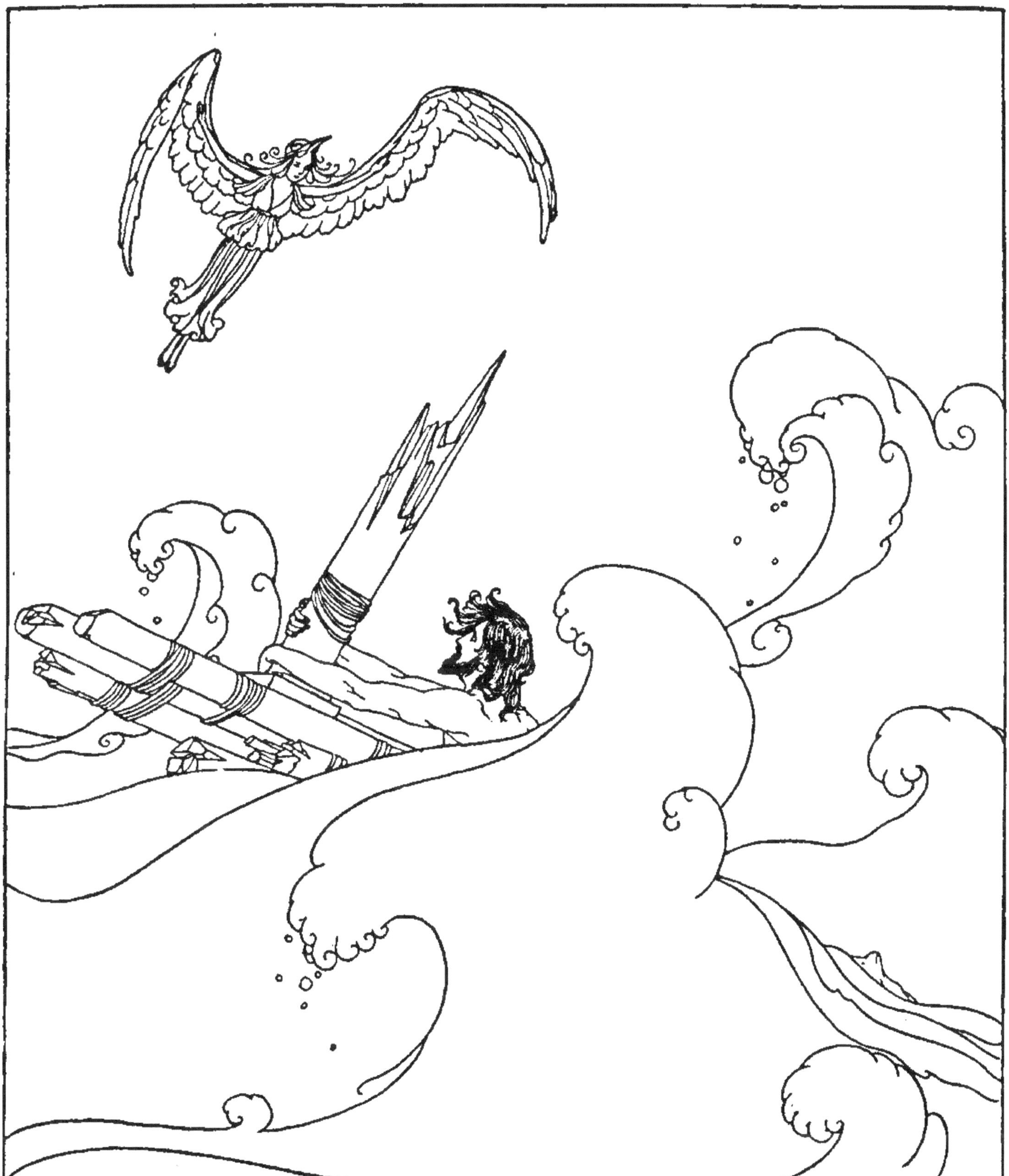

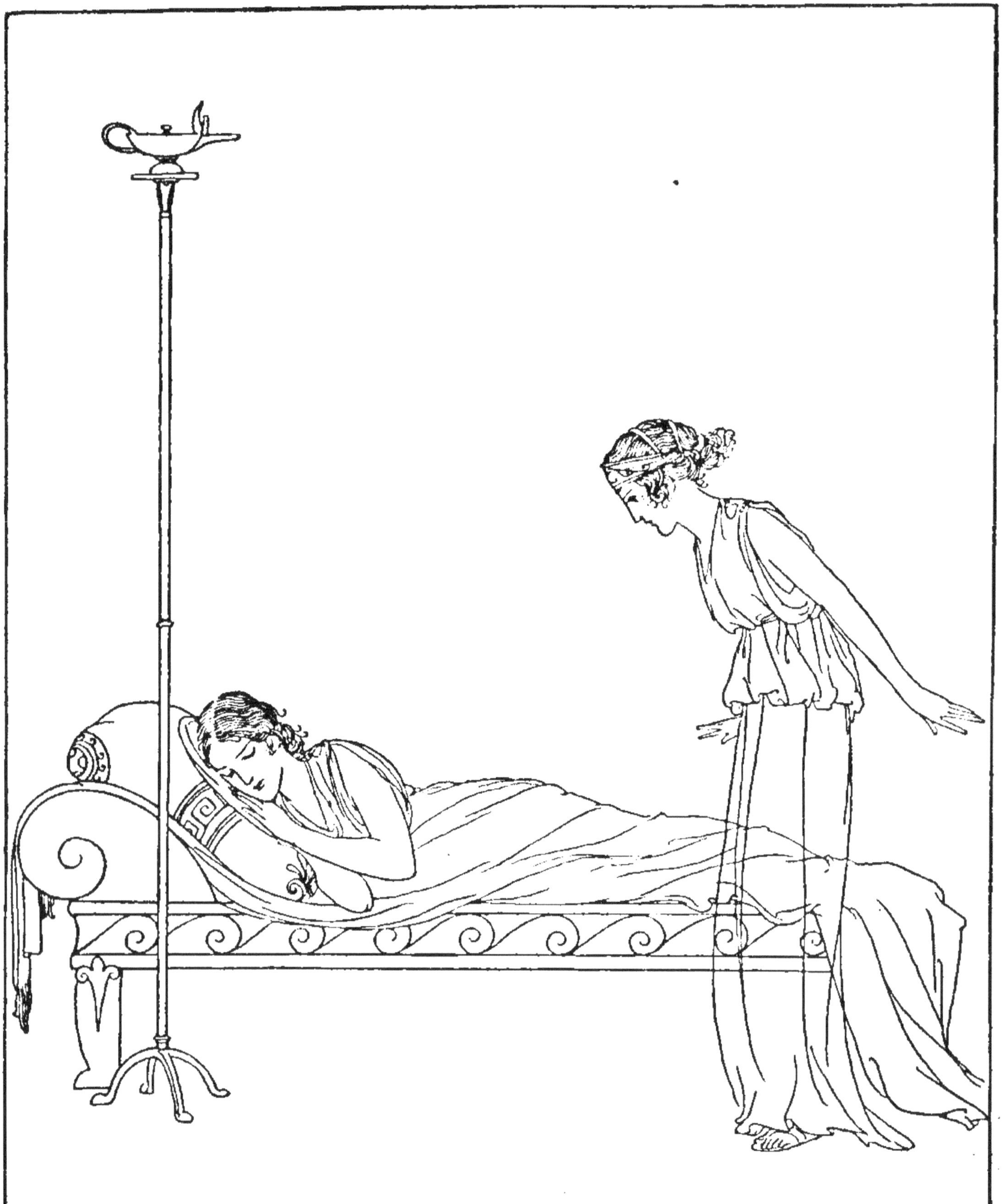

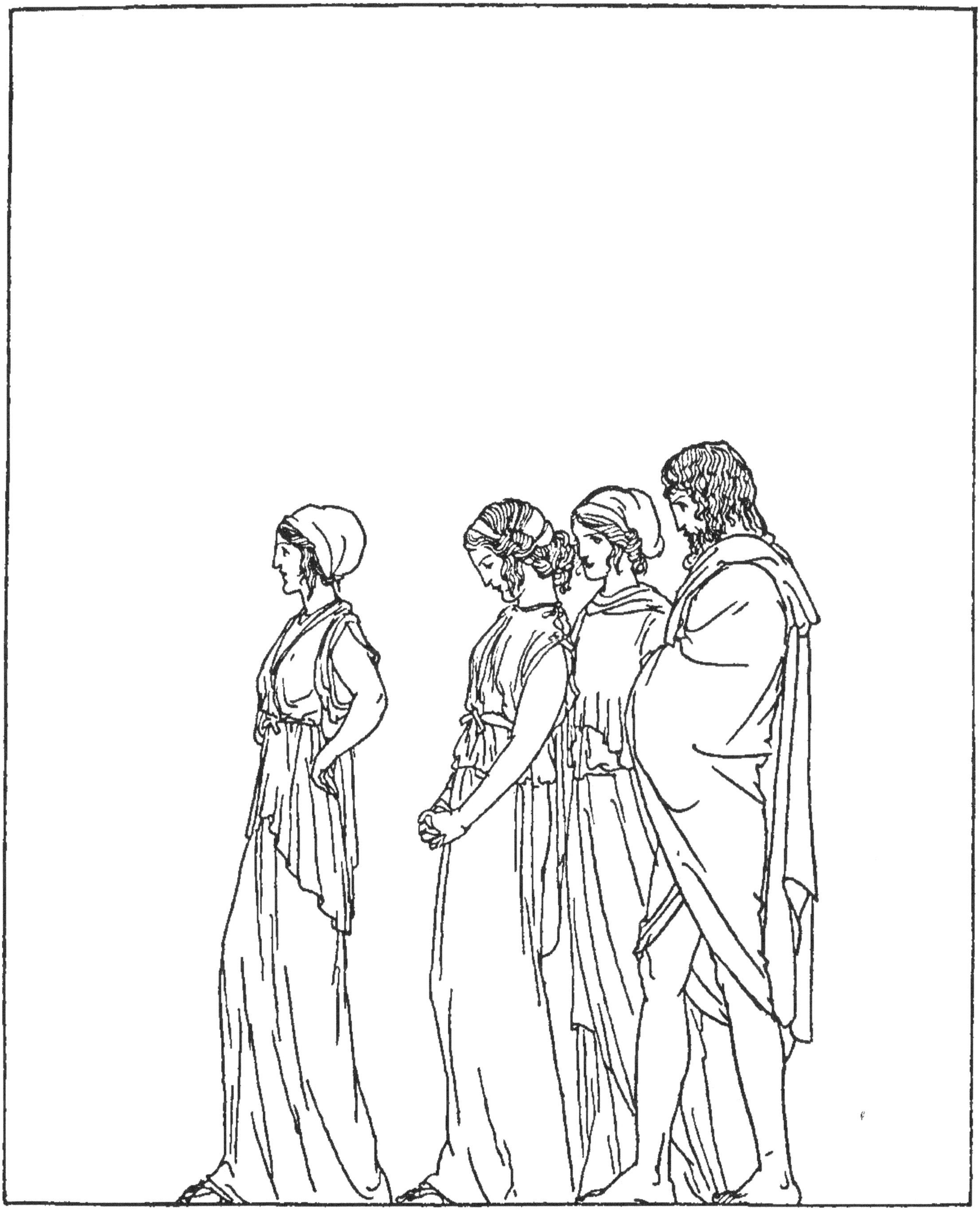

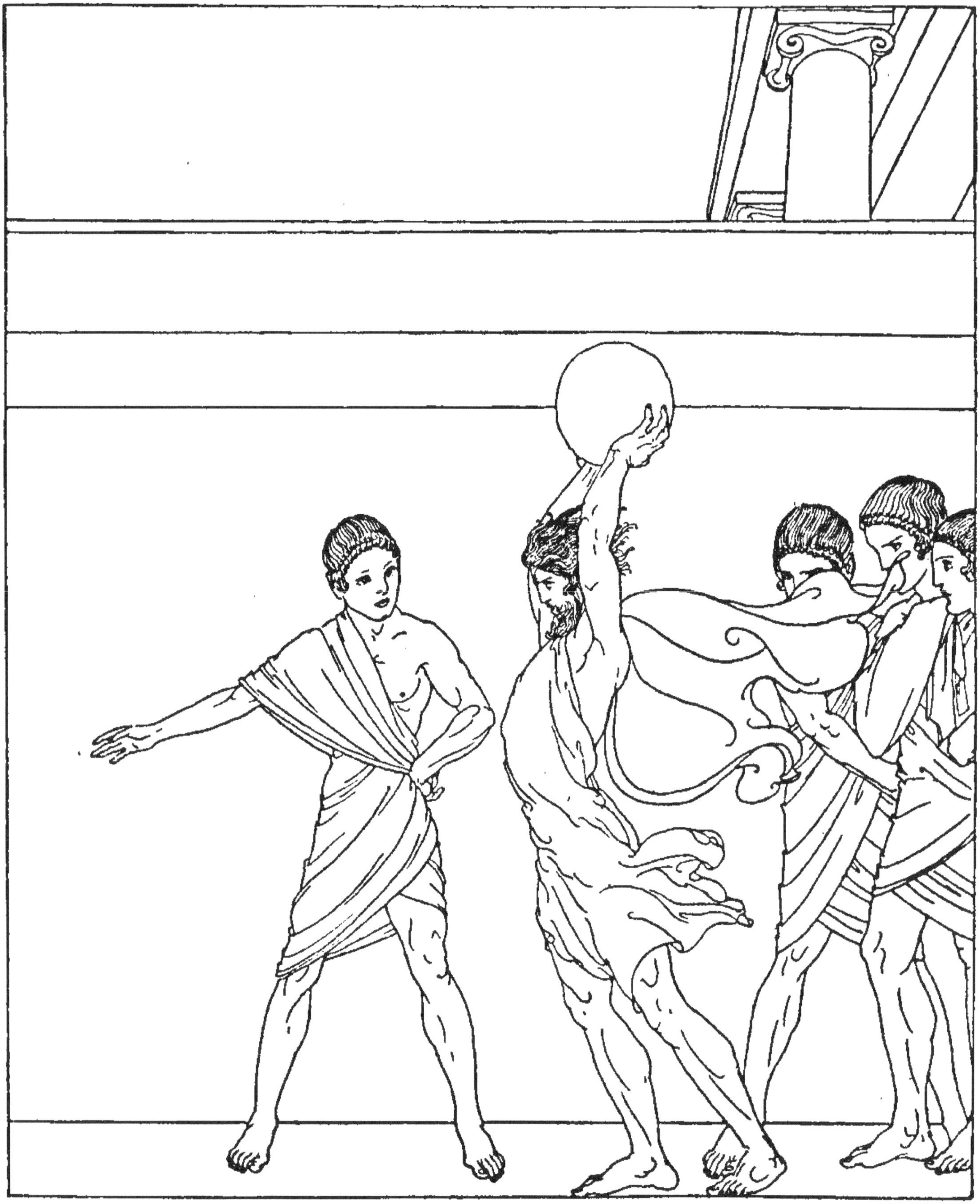

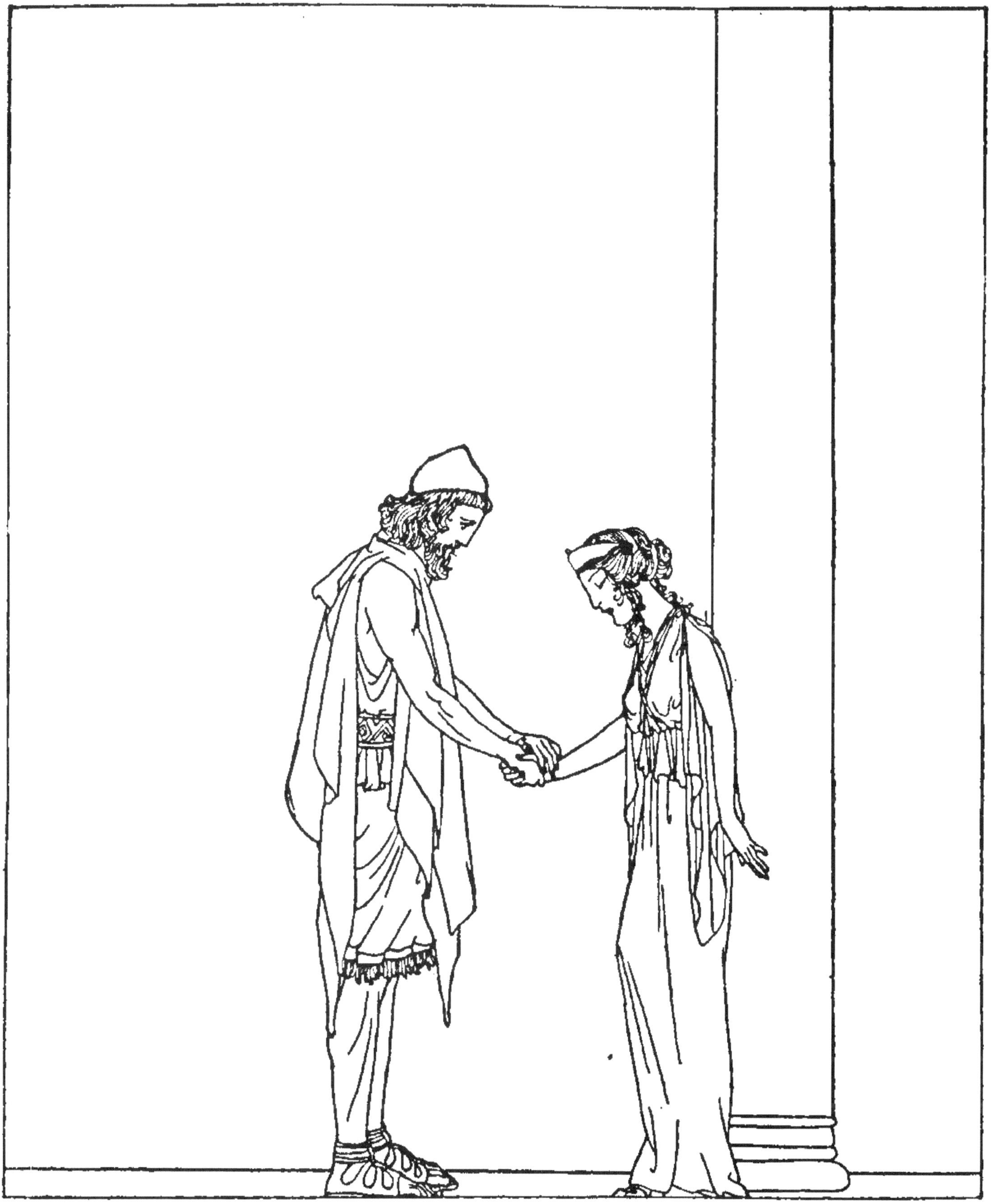

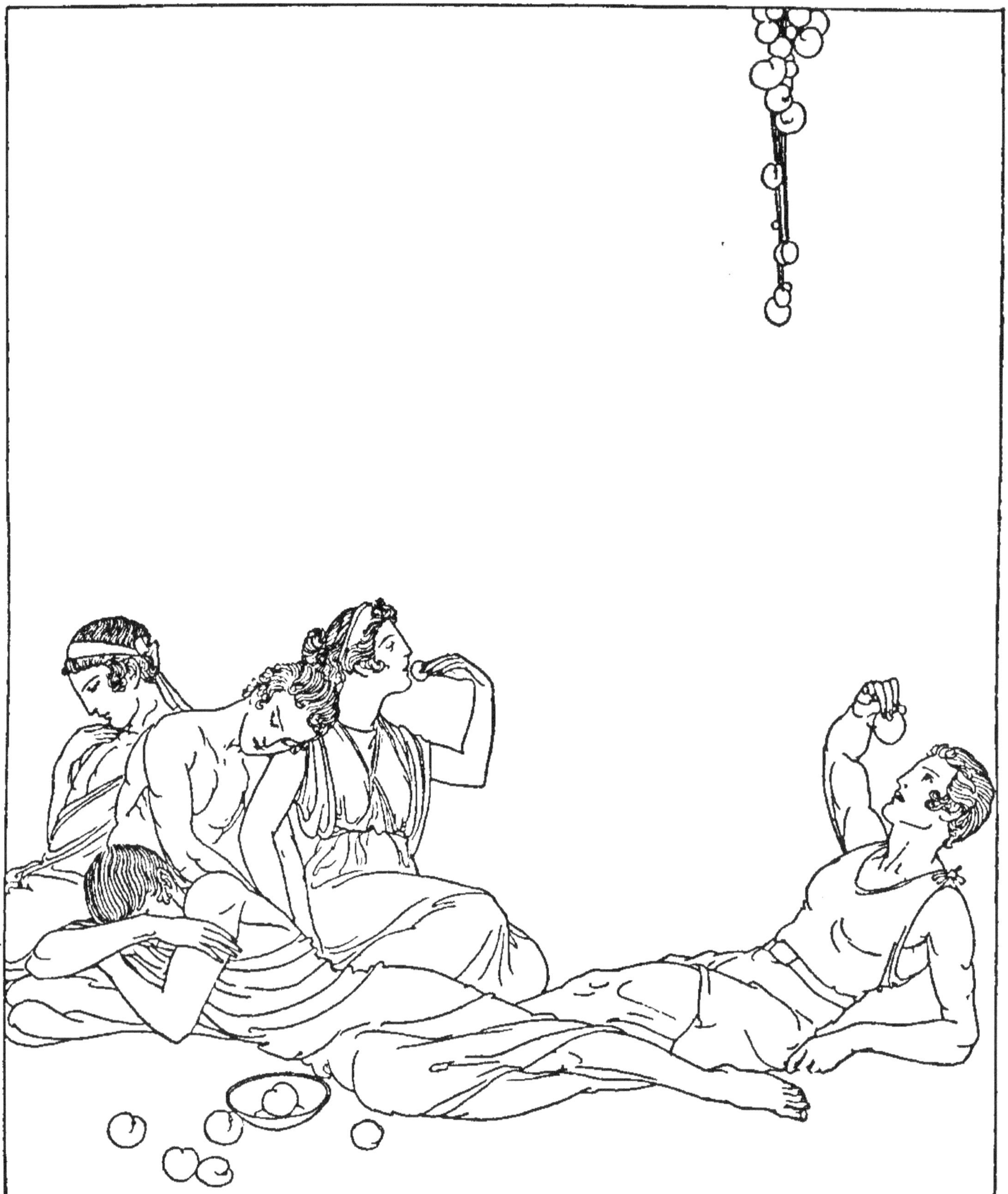

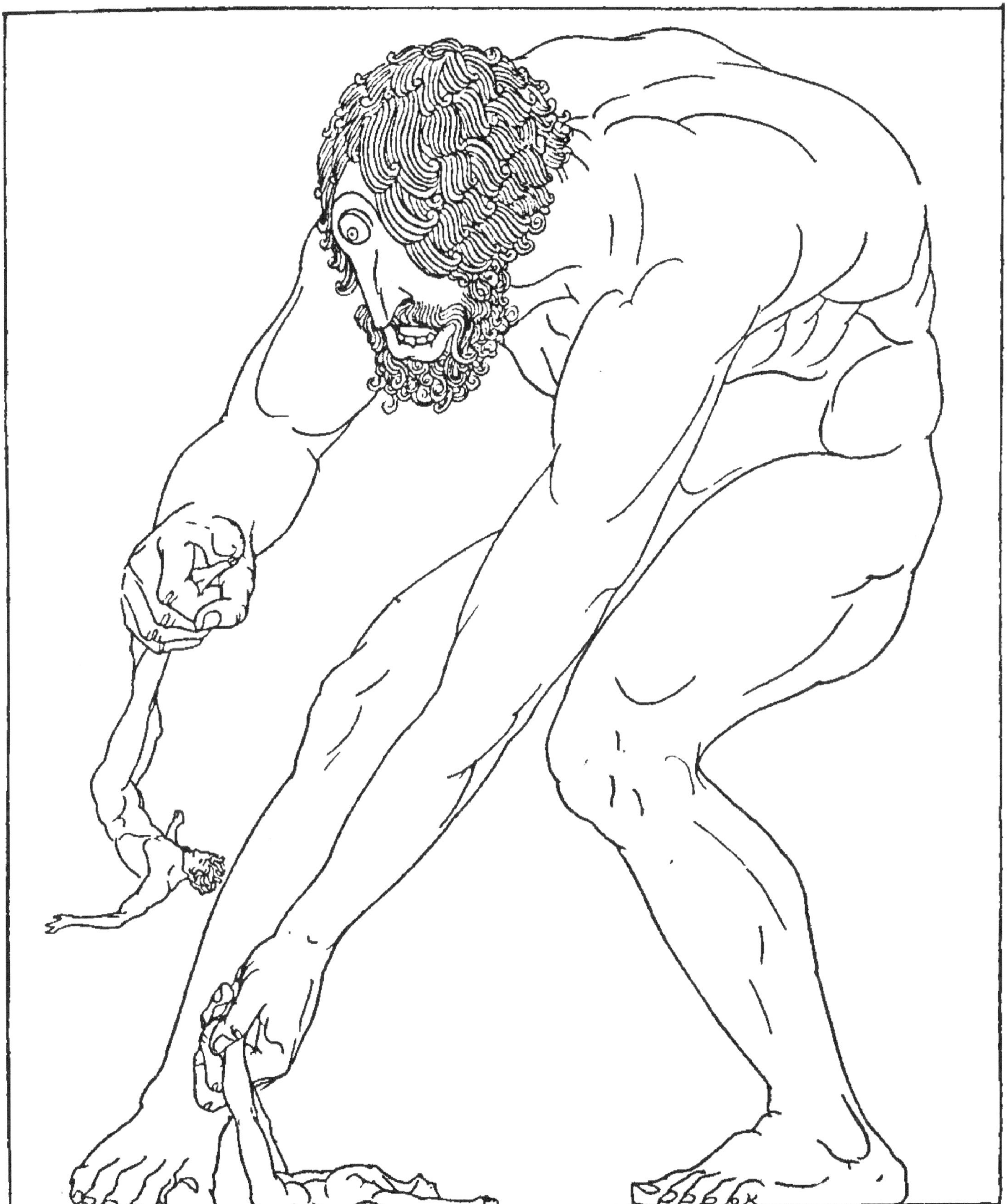

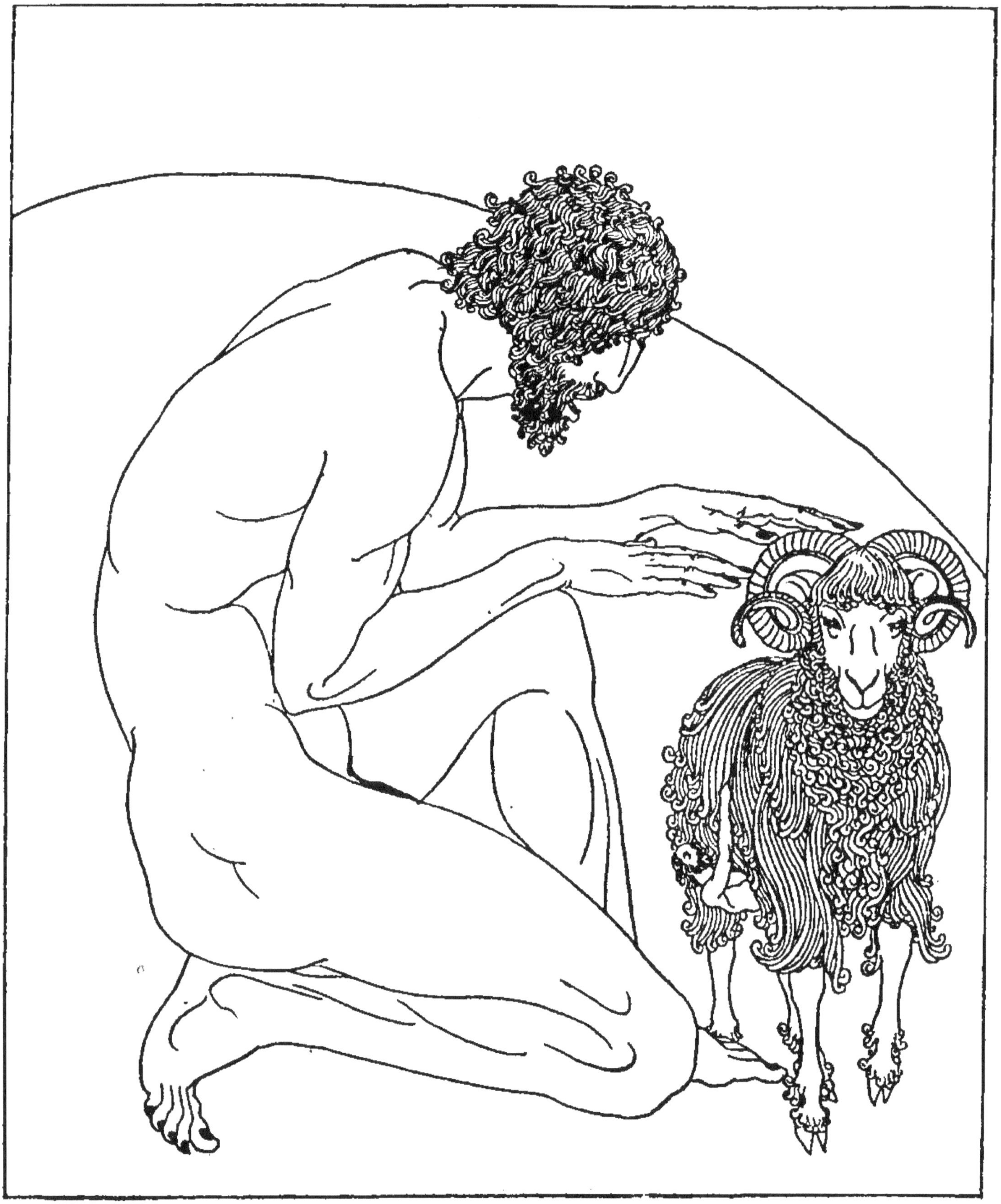

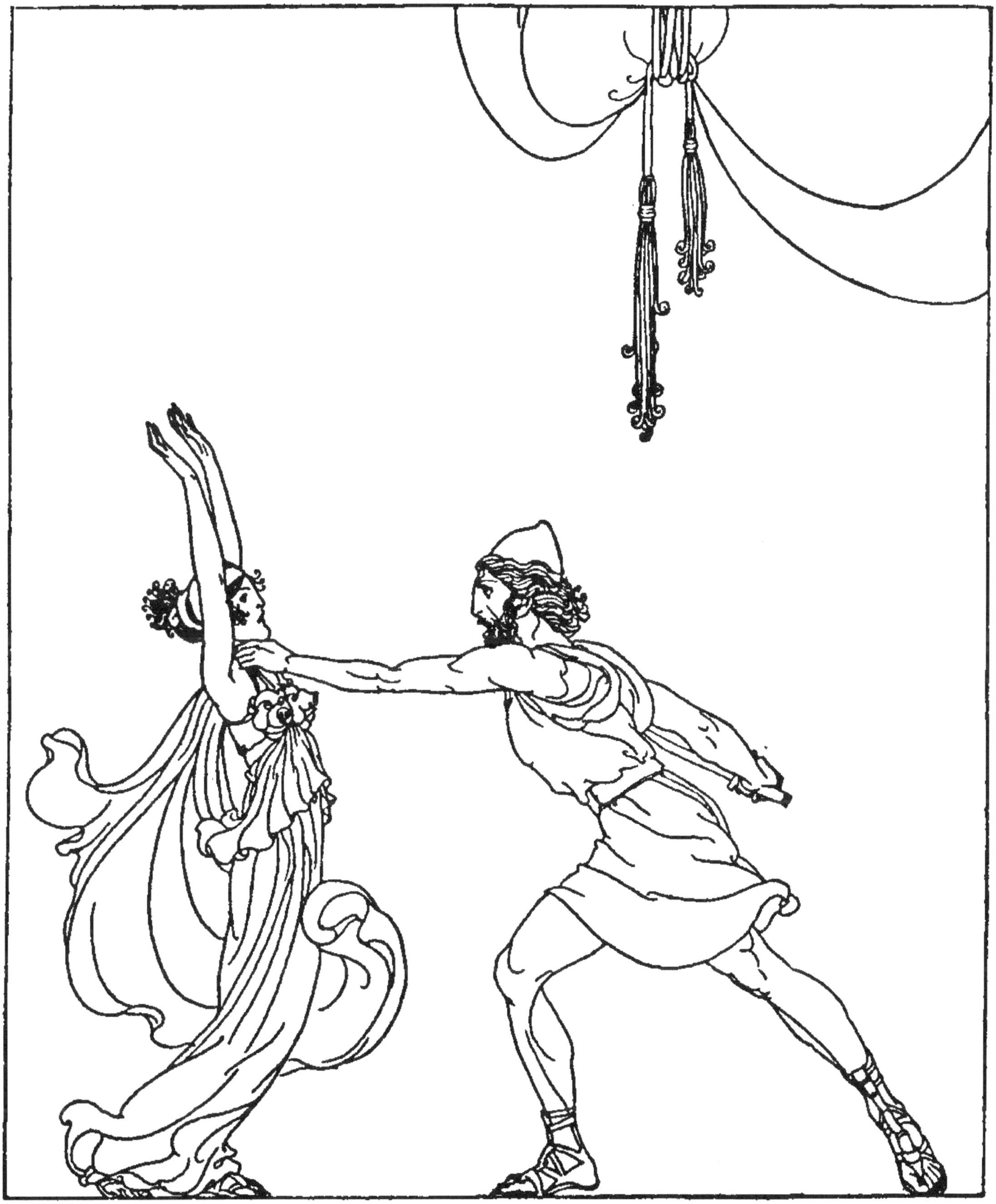

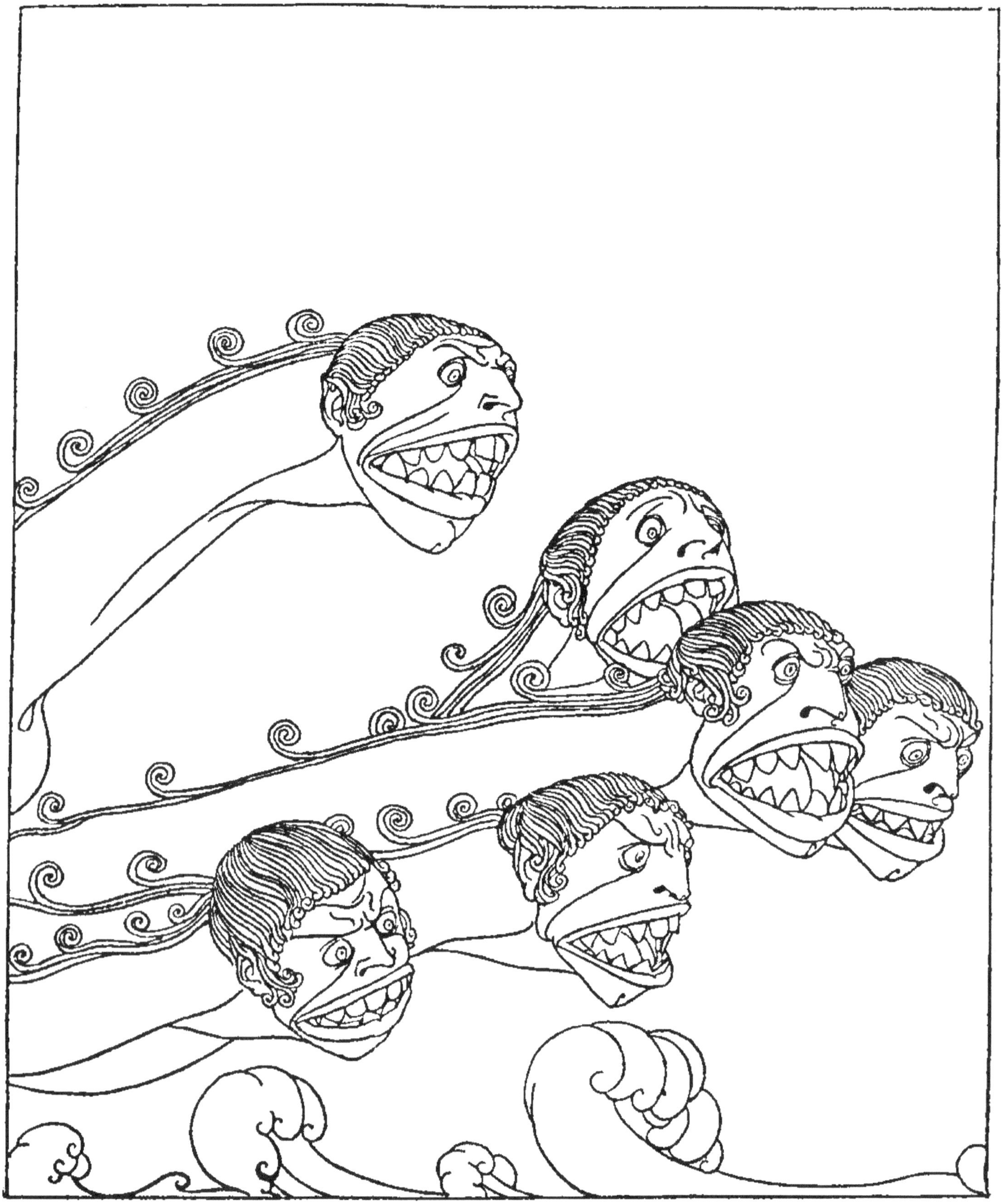

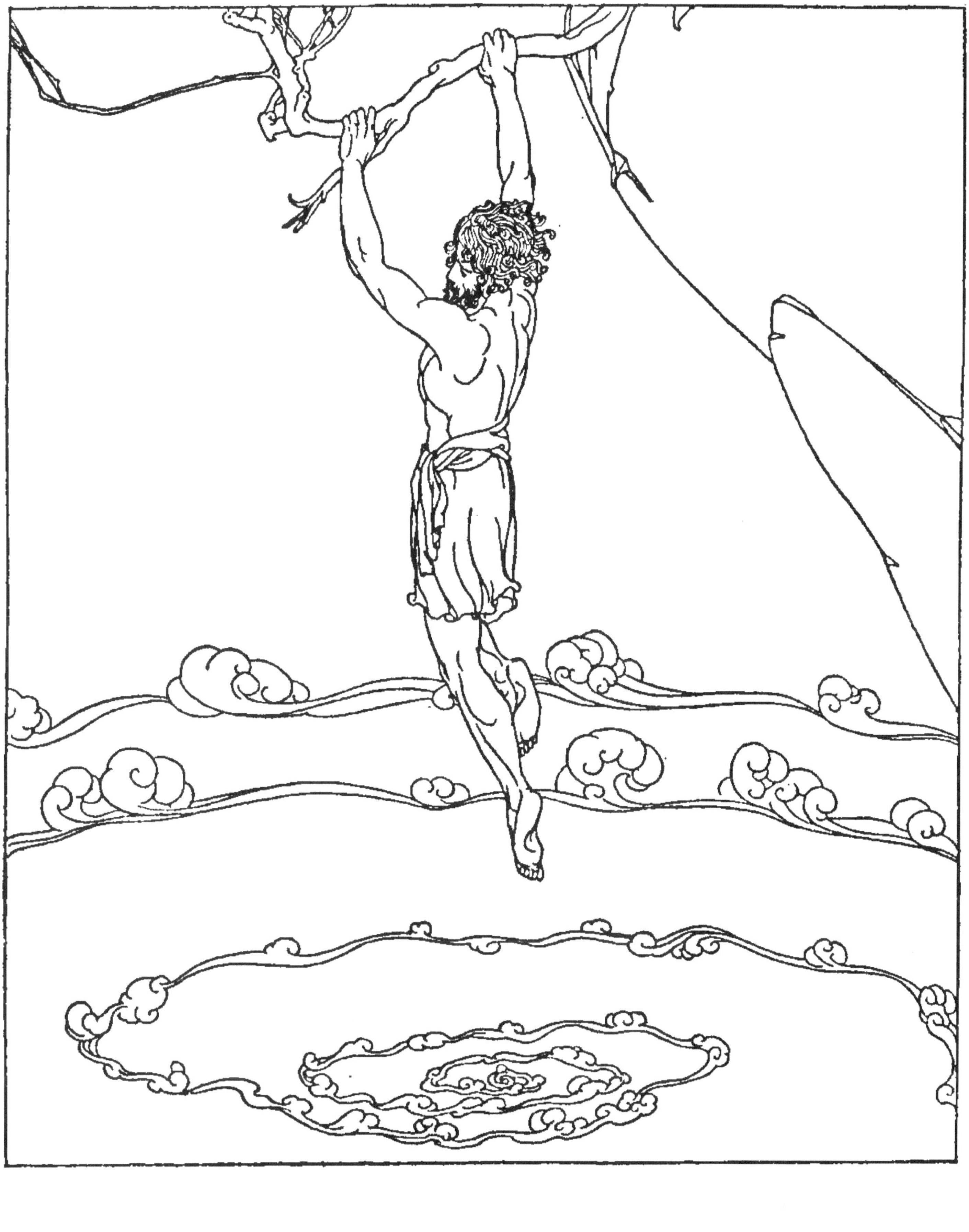

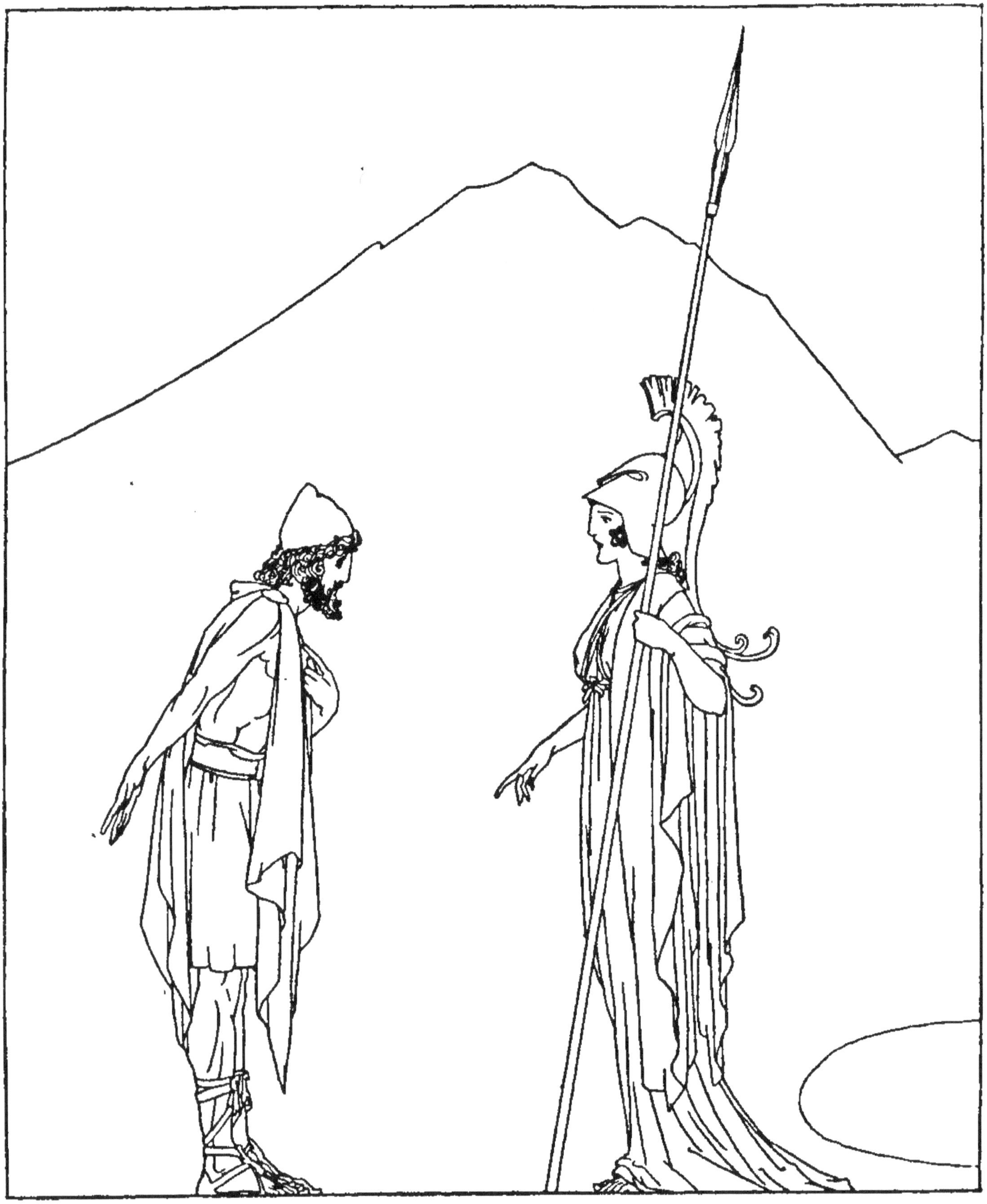

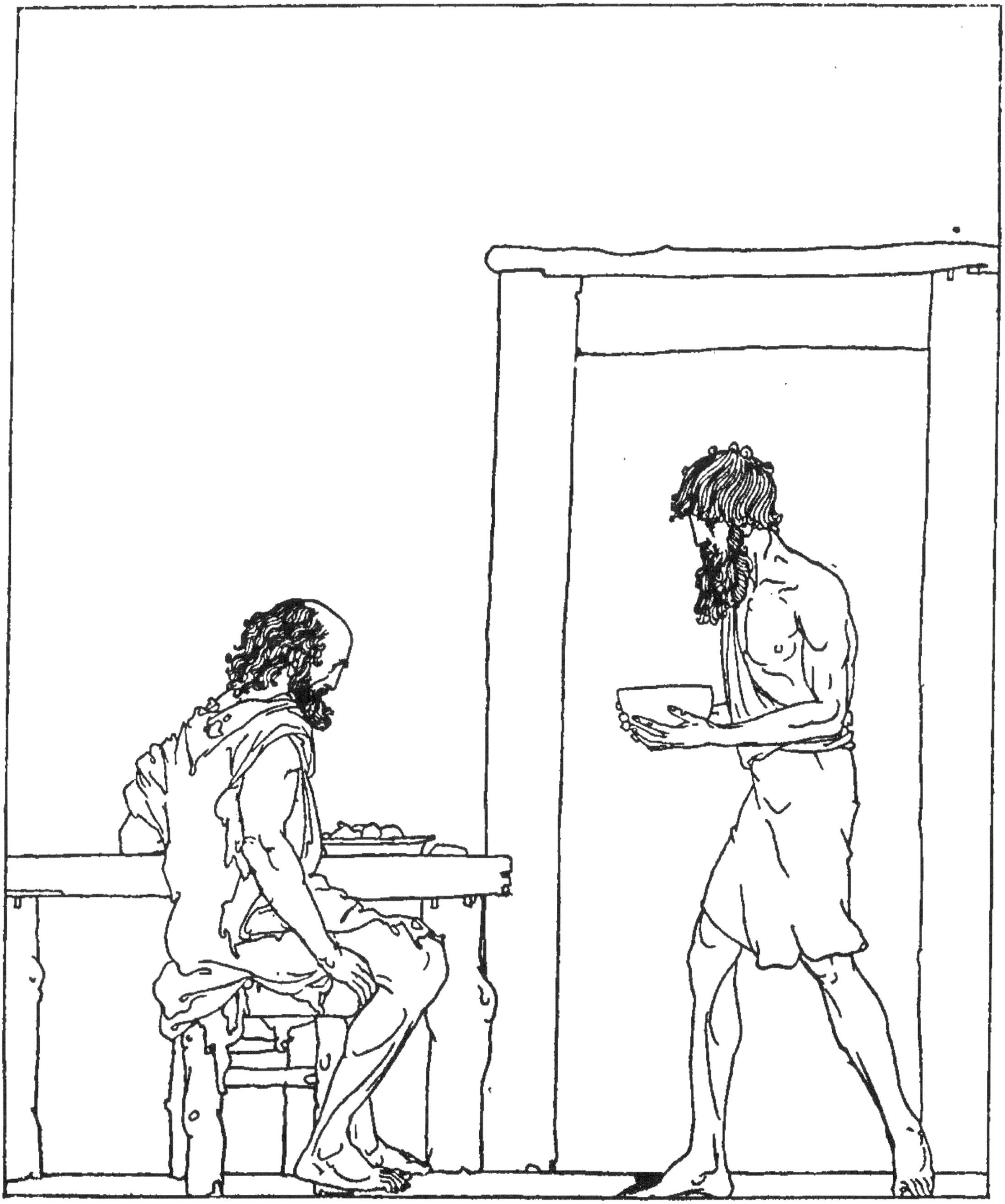

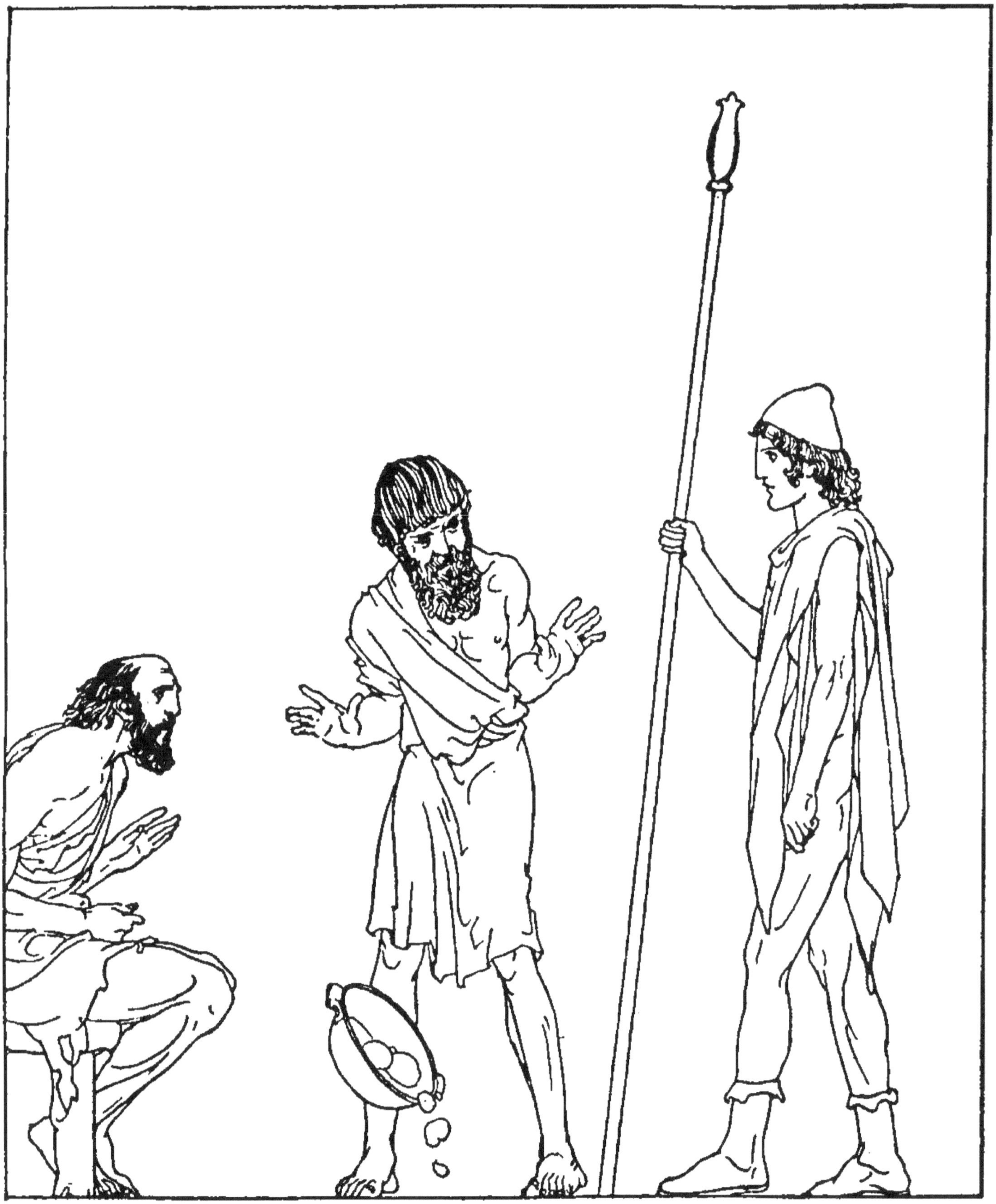

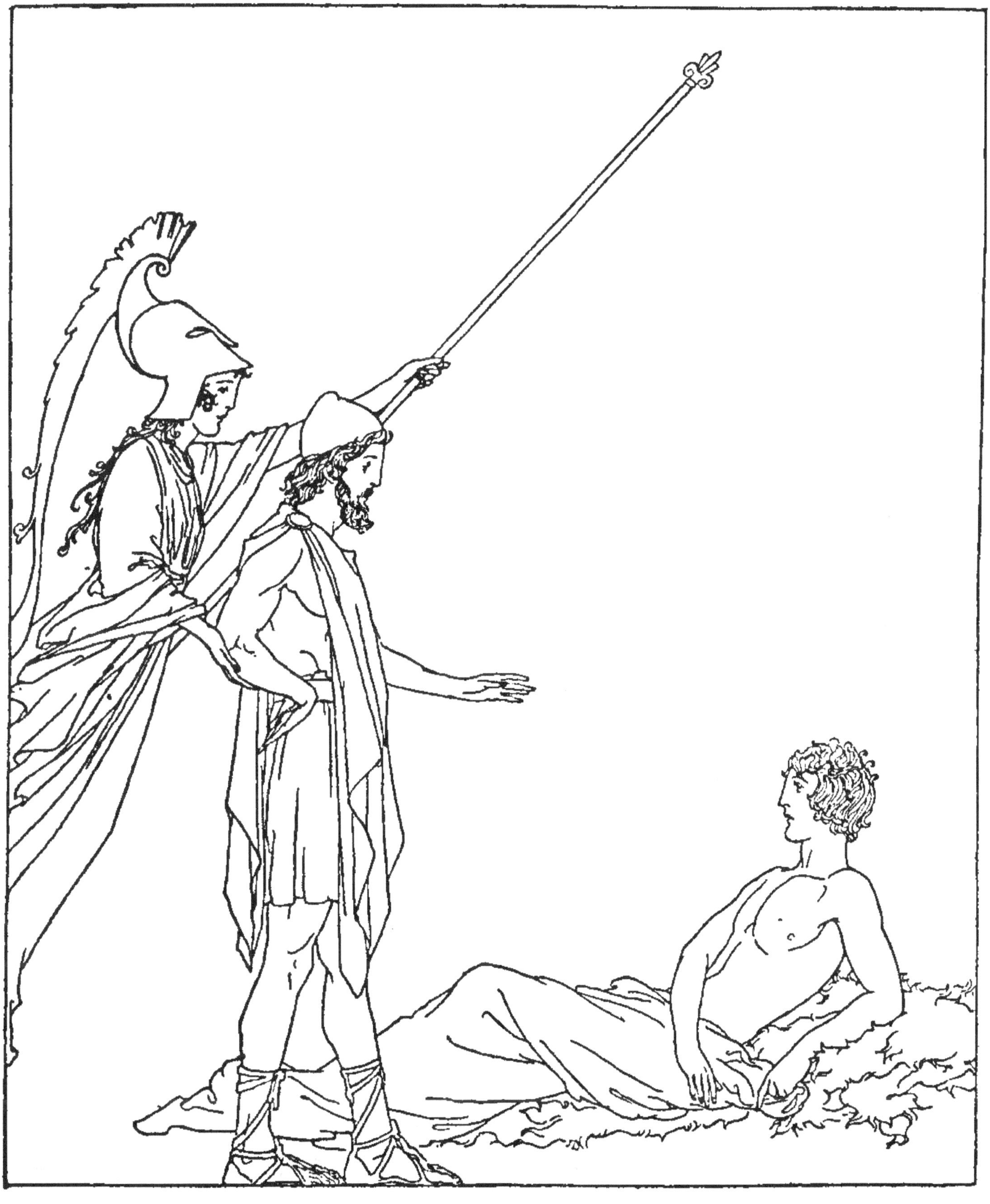

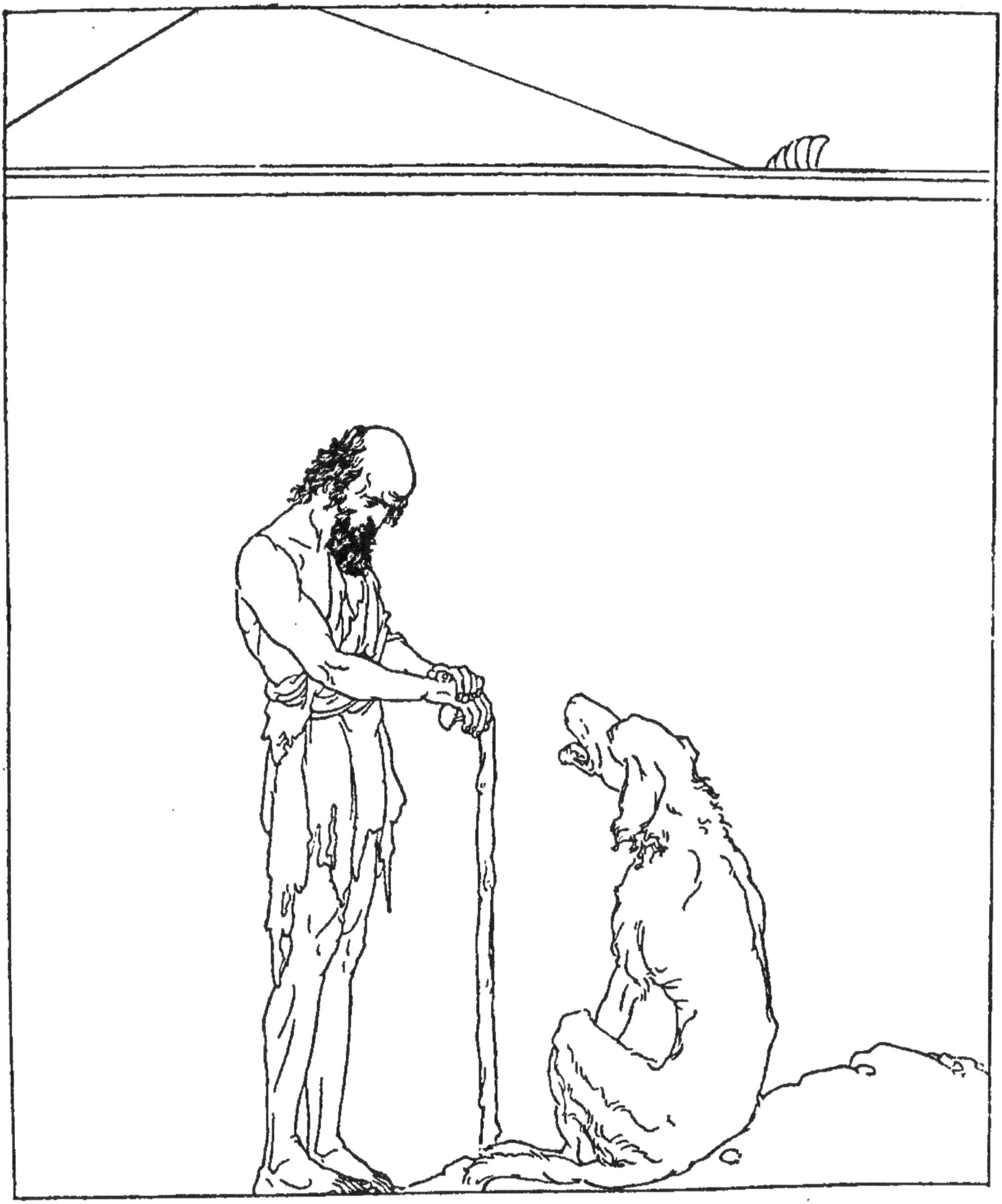

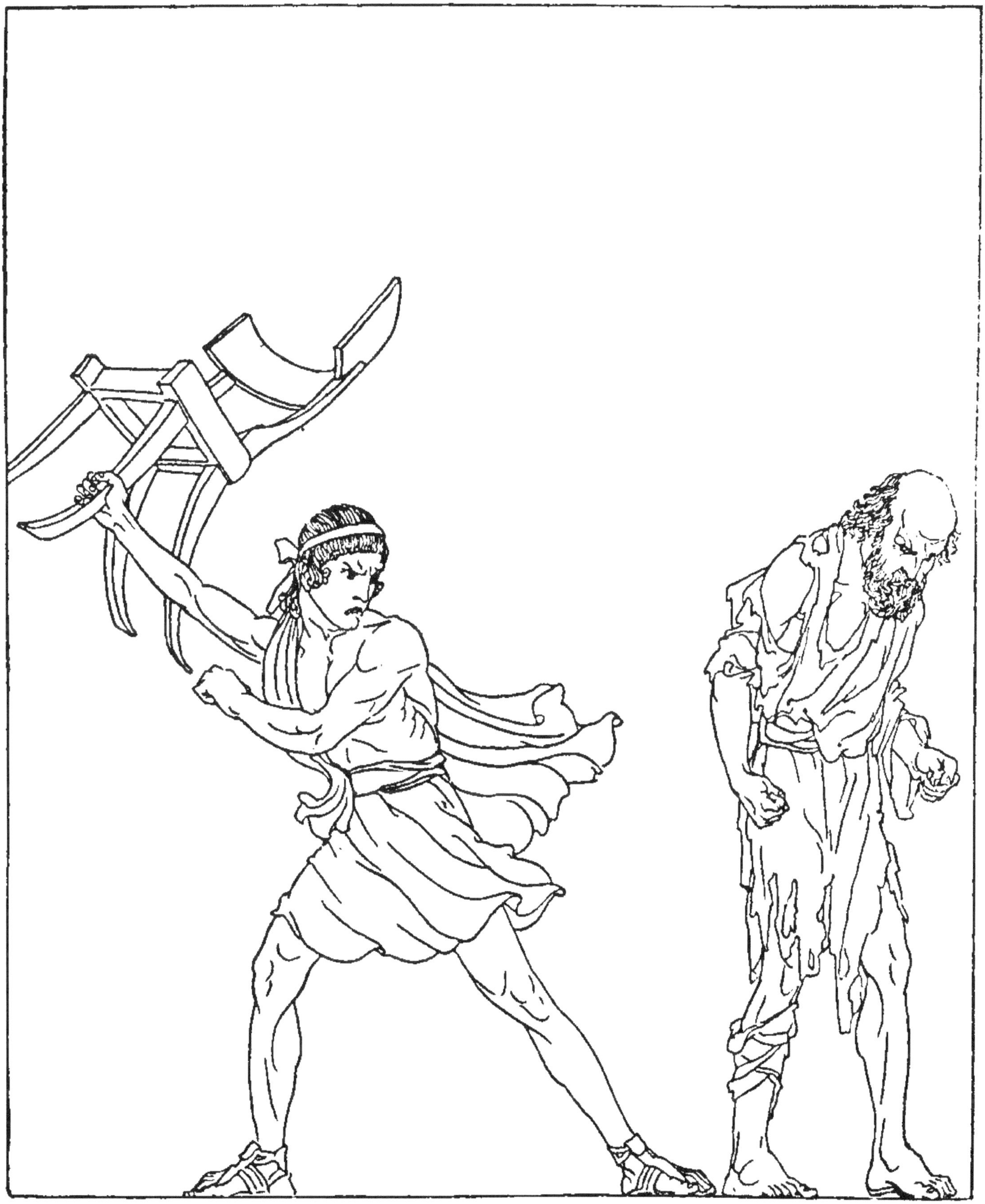

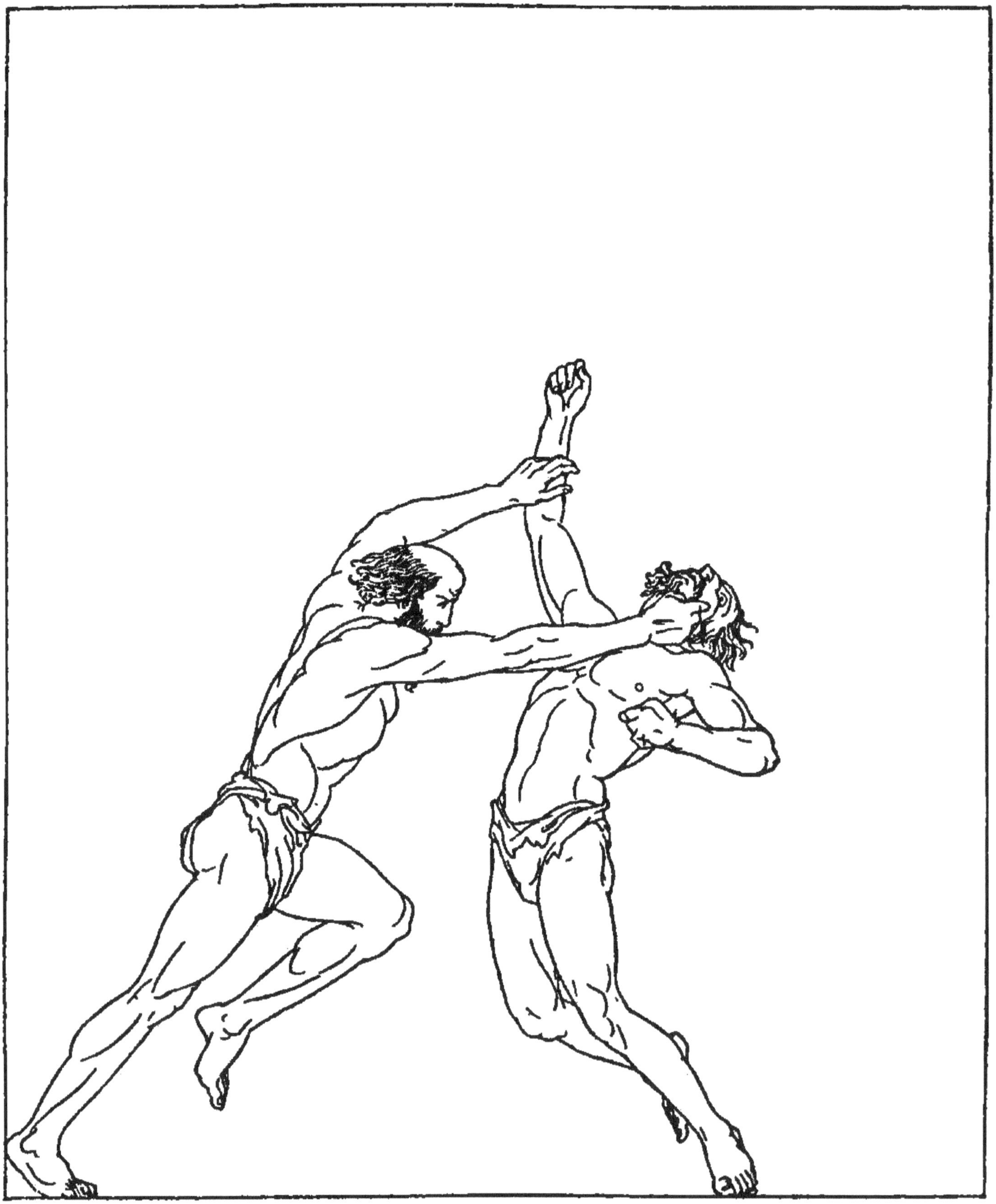

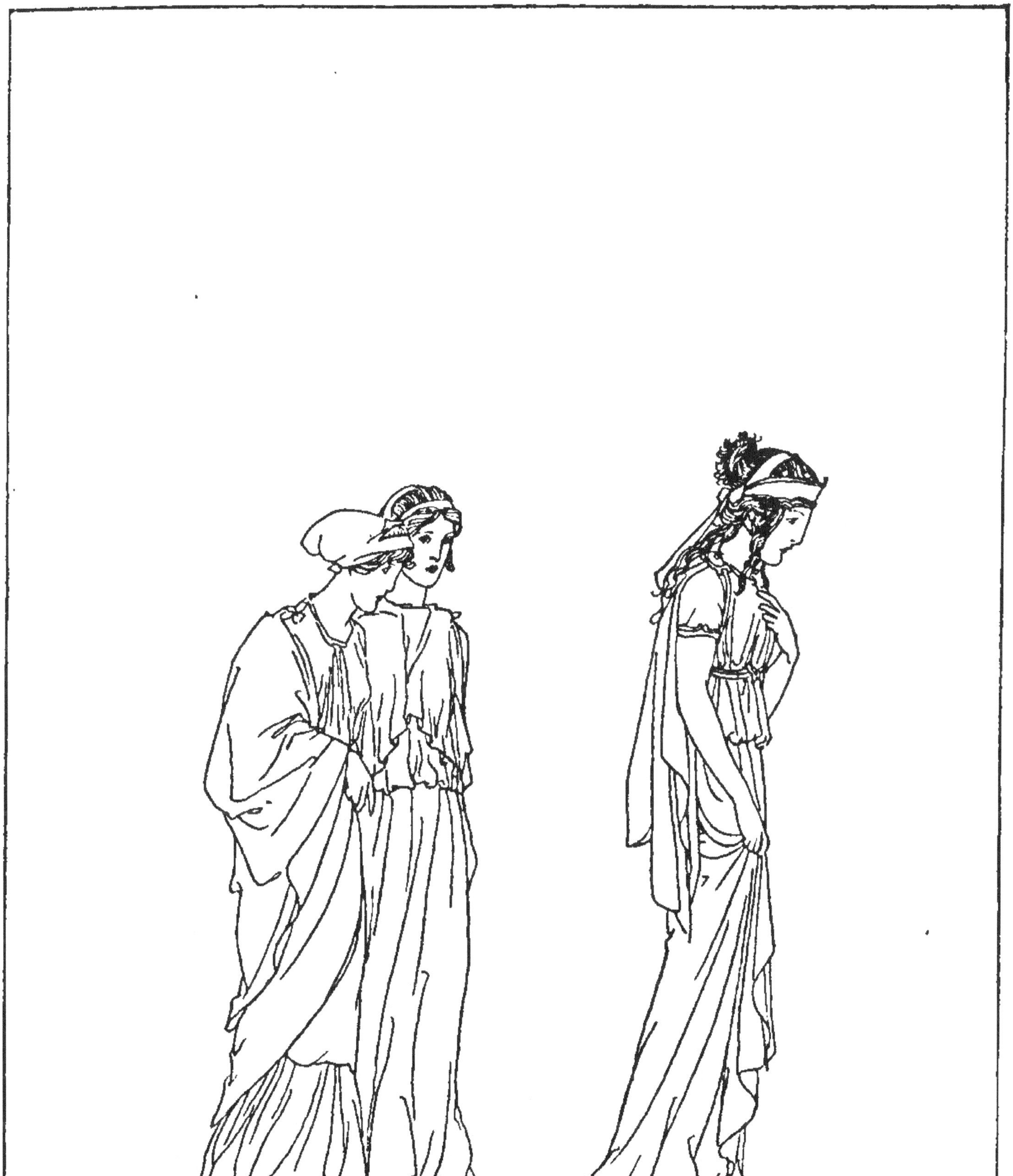

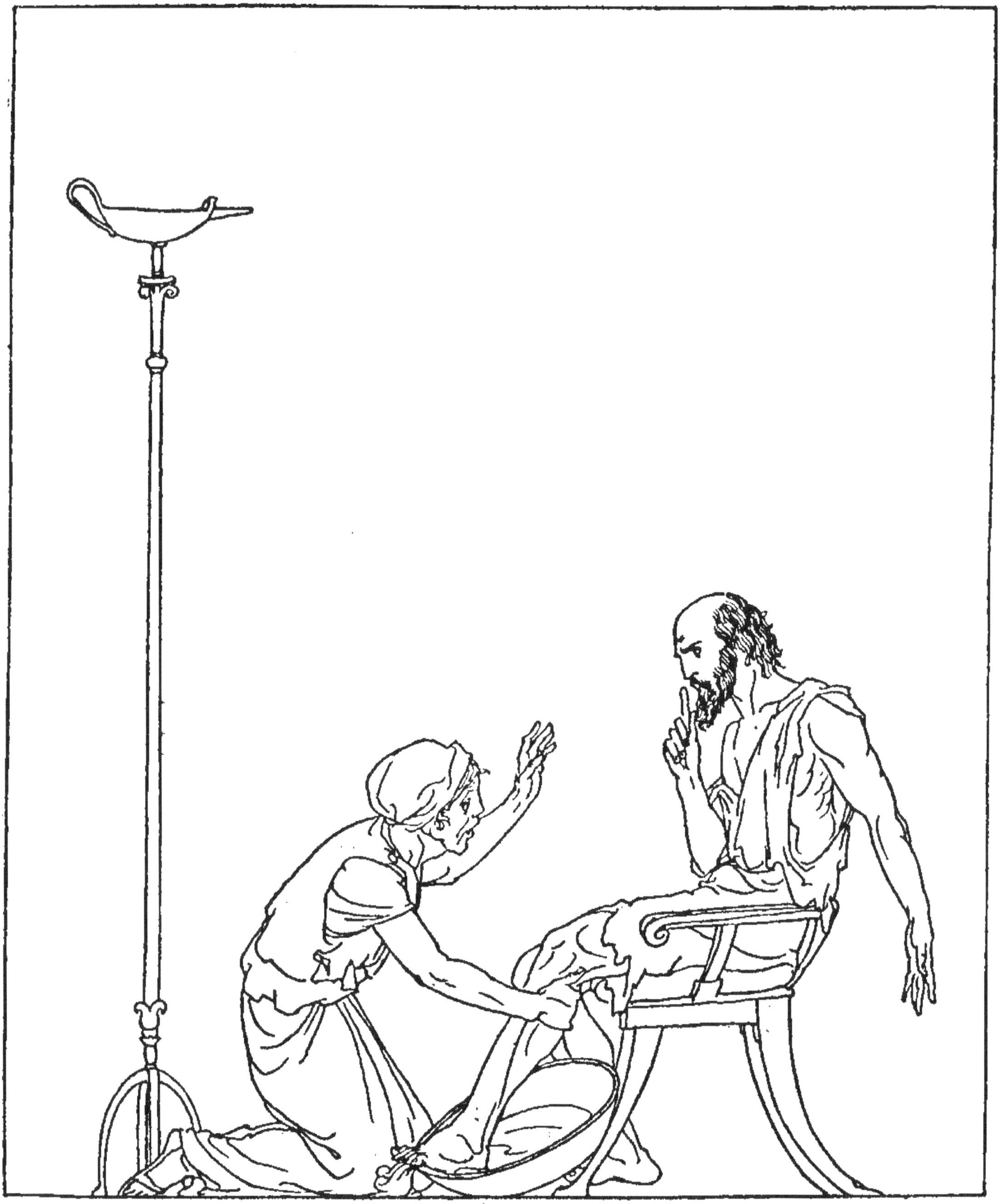

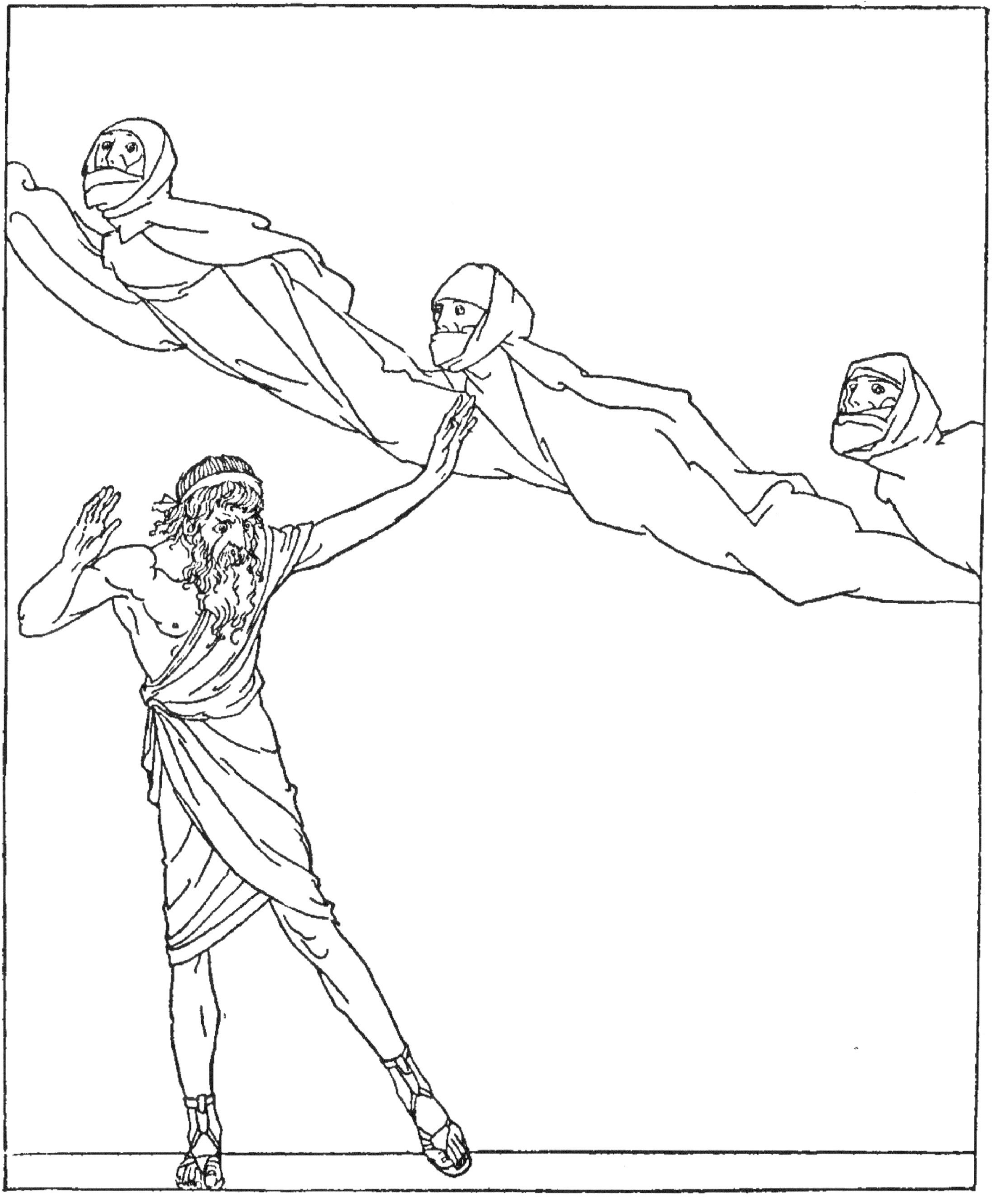

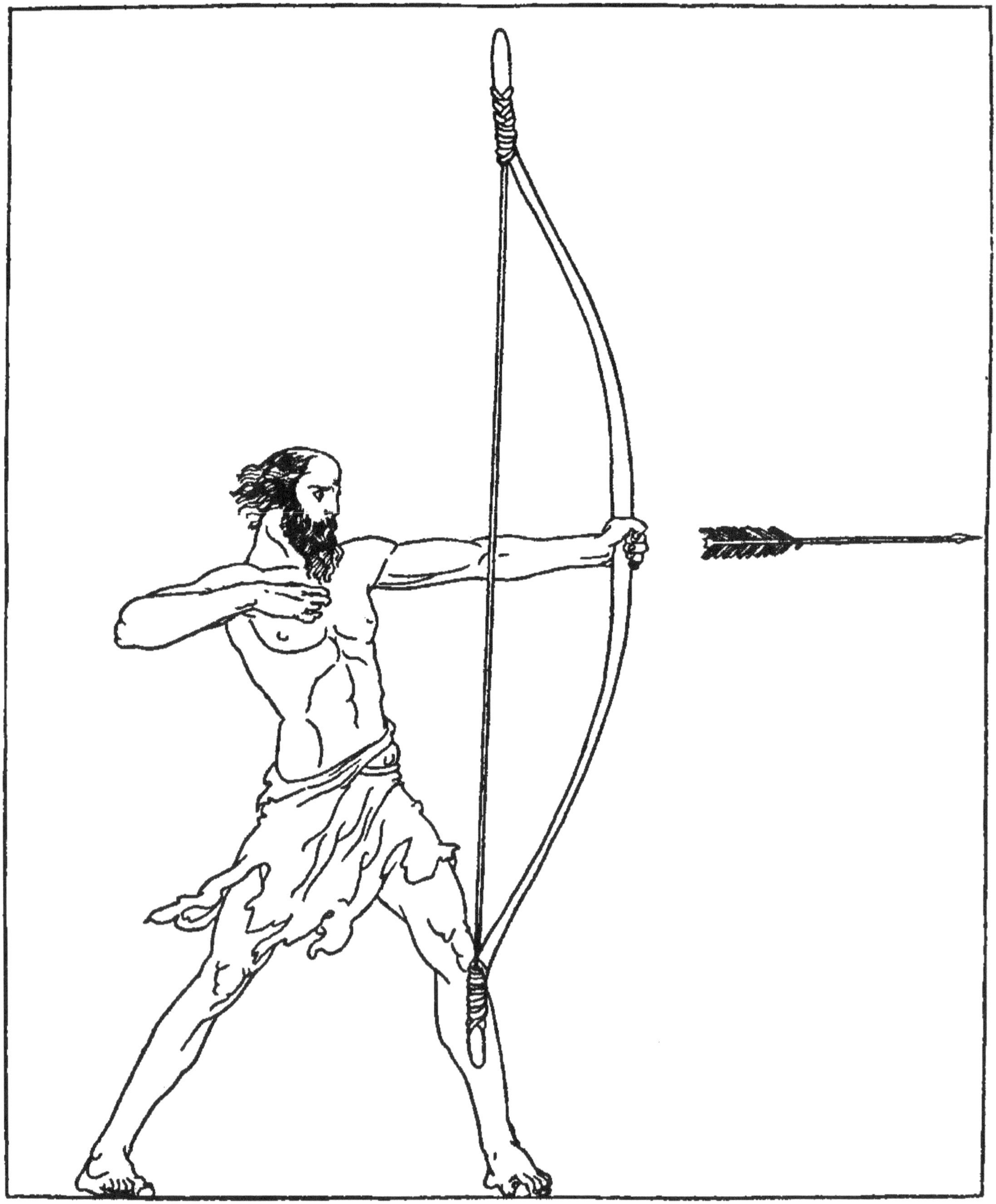

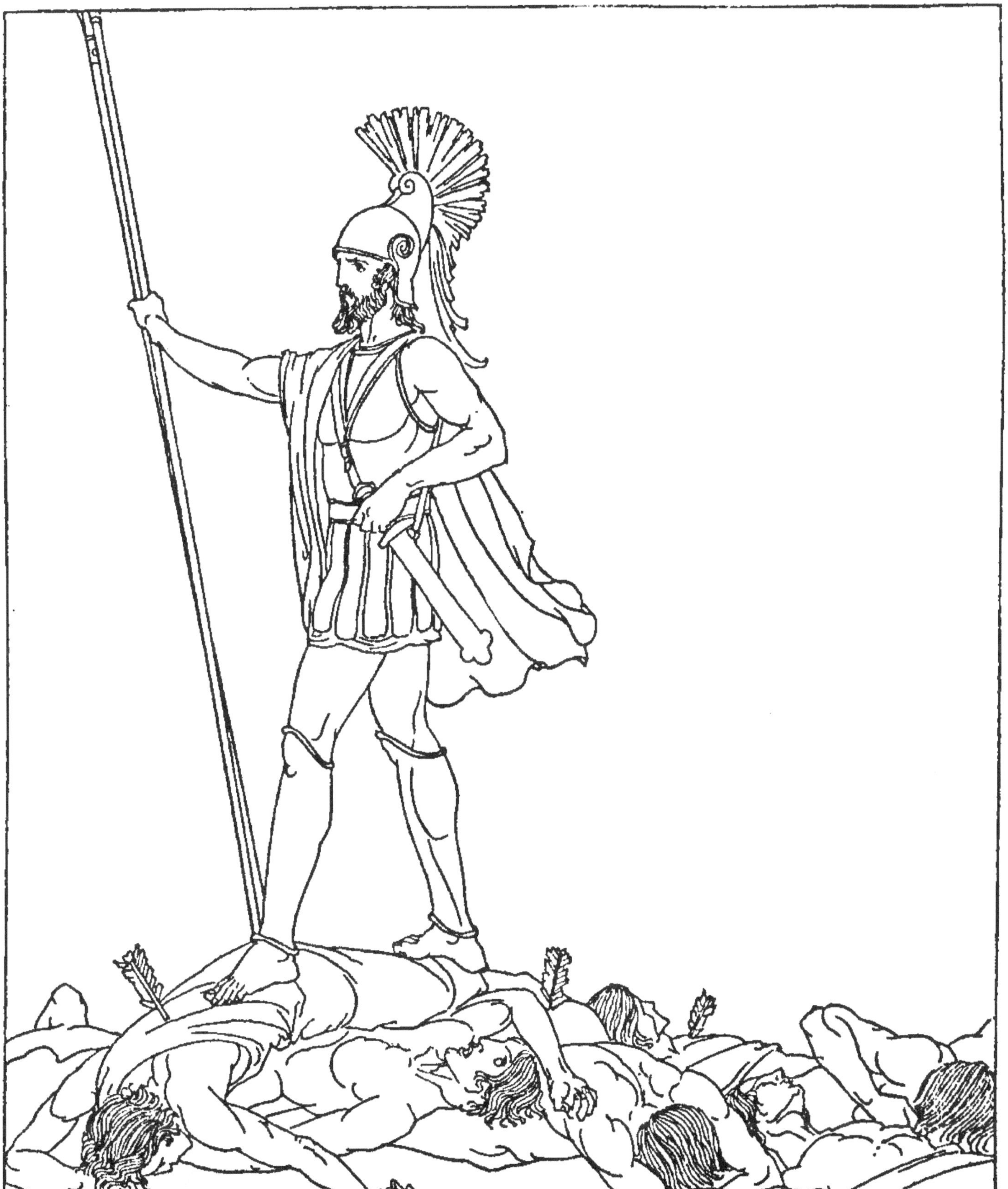

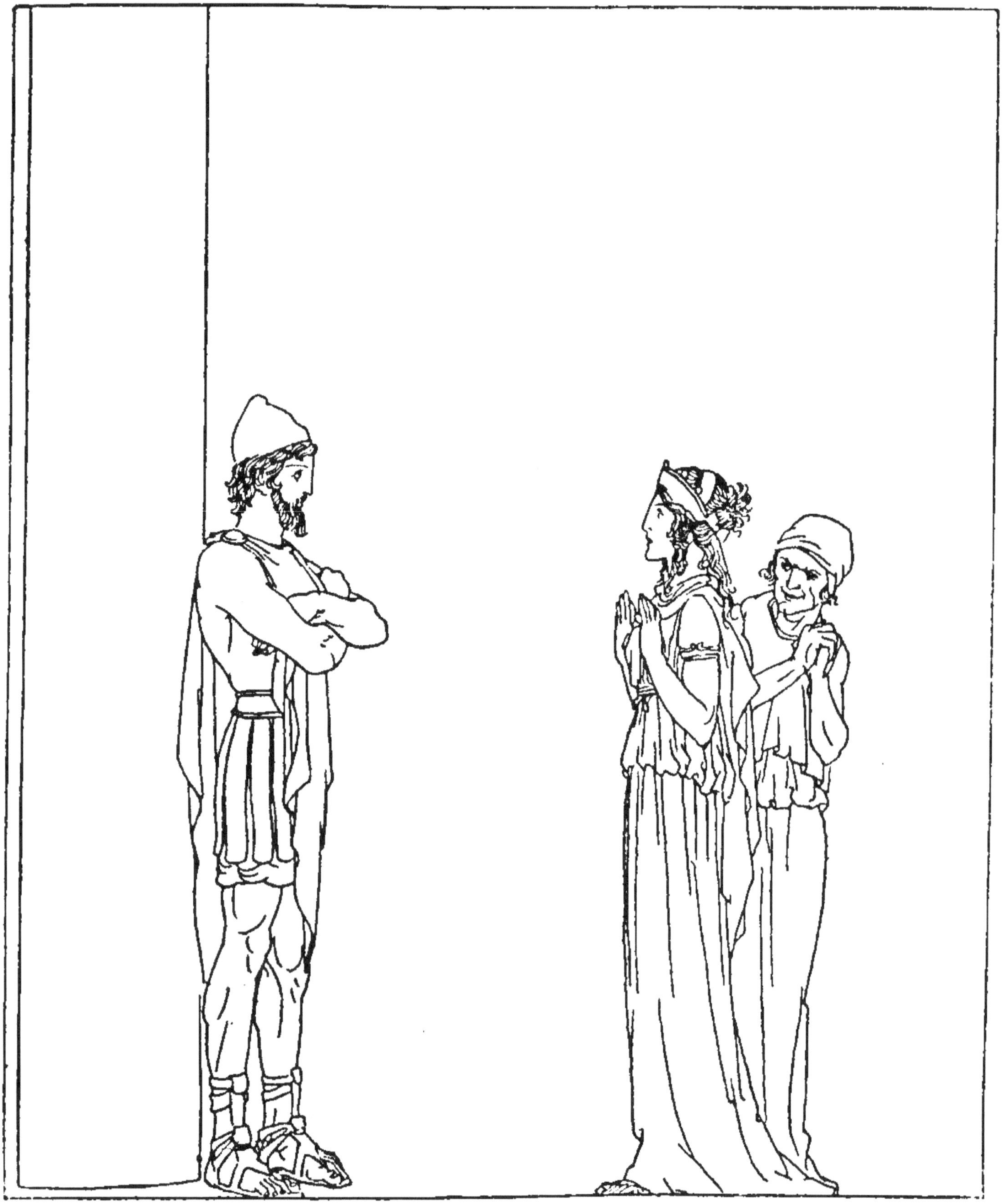

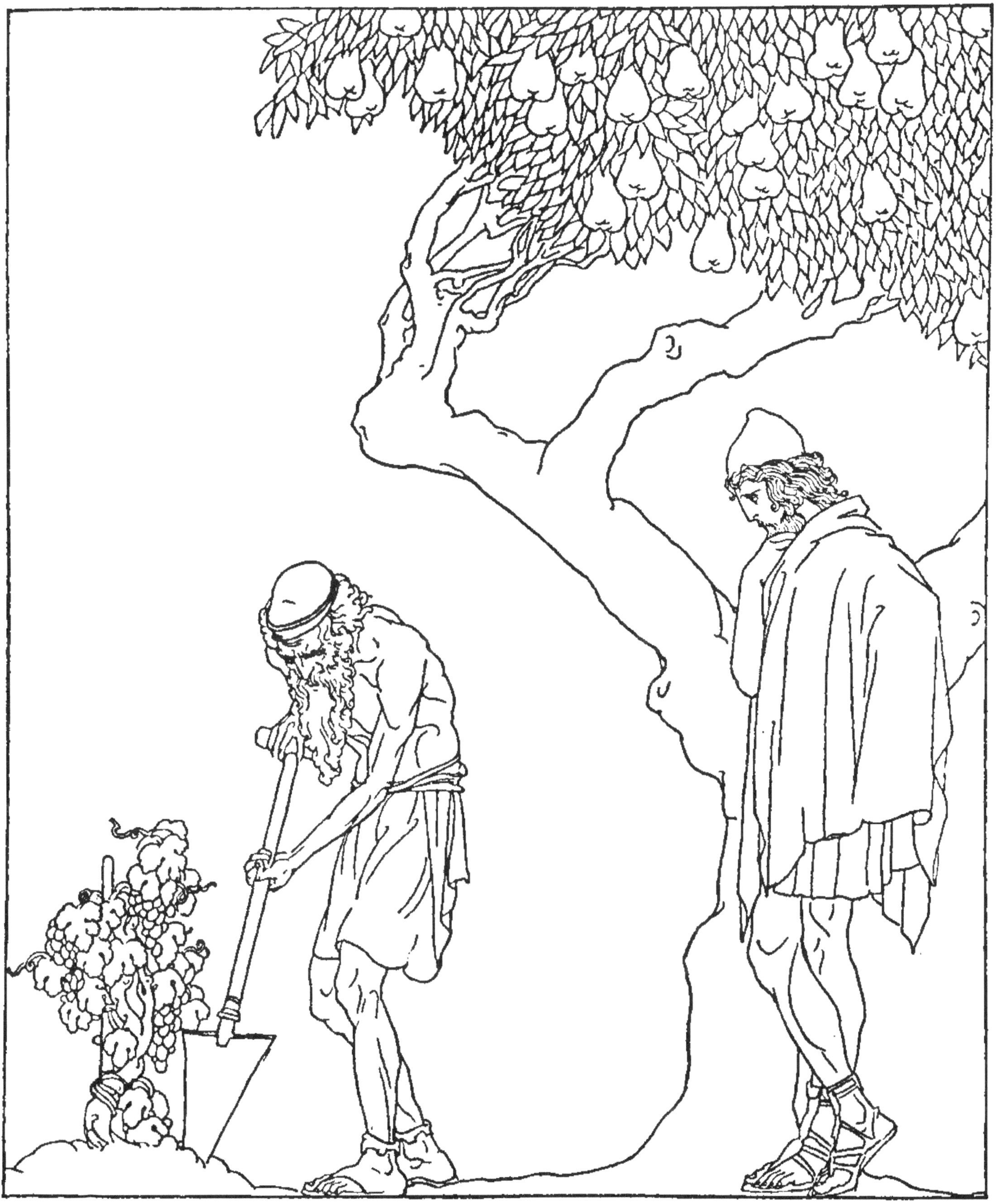

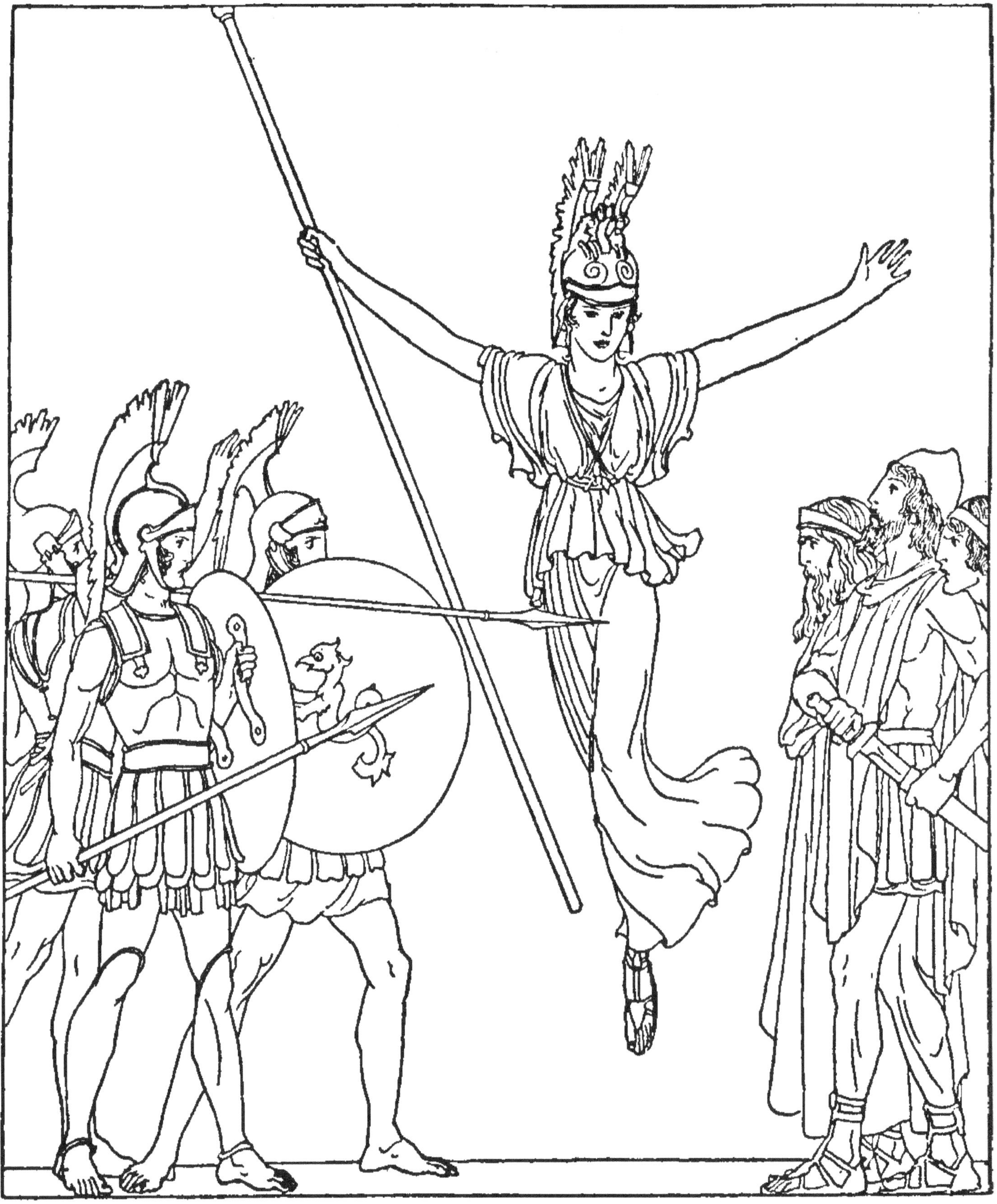

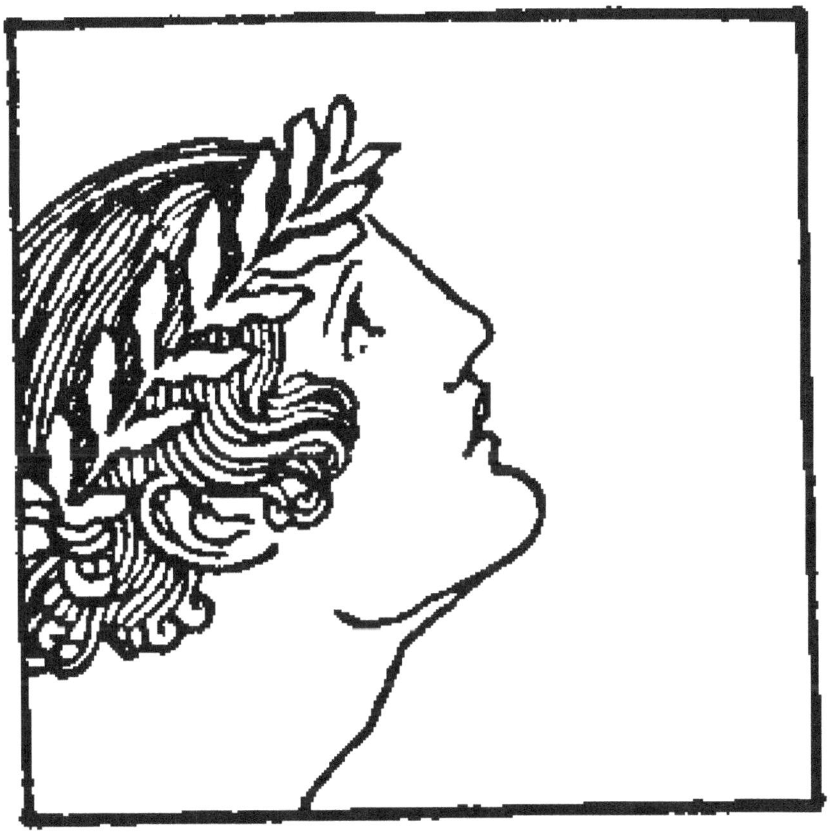

www.ingramcontent.com/pod-product-compliance
Lightning Source LLC
Chambersburg PA
CBHW082256220526
45469CB00009B/3022
* 9 7 8 1 7 2 5 6 4 9 6 5 1 *